now made by the prosecution. Defen[dant]
[th]at he is charged herein by his right nam[e]
[no]w states that his true name is Albert Haener. Defendants state
[th]ey are now ready to answer to said charge and each now pleads
[no]t guilty to said charge. Defendants now apply for and ask an ad-
[journ]ment of their examination herein until 10 oclock A.M. on the 24th
[da]y of June A.D. 1893 and it being made to appear there is a necessity
[for] such adjournment it is ordered that these proceedings be adjourn-
[ed] to said last named hour and day, that defendants are required to
[th]en be and appear herein before me for further proceedings and
[ex]amination respecting said charge, that they do give bail for their
[sa]id appearance herein at that time each in the sum of four hun-
[dr]ed dollars and in default of said bail they be and stand commit-
[t]ed to the jail of said county until the said time to which these pro-
[ce]edings are adjourned and at that time to be then brought before
[m]e. The Defendants now each give bail in said sum by recog-
[n]izance in due form signed by their sureties Leonard Short and
[E]li A. Signor for each of them and thereupon defendants are released
[fr]om custody.

[J]une 23rd 1893. M.C. Brown Attorney for the prosecution makes
[ap]plication for a subpoena for David Stewart. Otto Franc, John Chapman,
[Da]vid Blanchard and James Thomas as witnesses for the state. Subpoena
[iss]ued and delivered to John B Houghton Constable who on this day
[re]turns herein said Subpoena as served personally by him on each of
[sa]id Witnesses at Lander in said County.

Butch Cassidy, My Brother

I hope you enjoy learning about Butch's life as much as
I've enjoyed telling it.

Lula Parker Betenson

My brother, Robert LeRoy Parker (Butch Cassidy).

Butch Cassidy, My Brother

Lula Parker Betenson
as told to
Dora Flack

Brigham Young University Press
Provo, Utah

Library of Congress Cataloging in Publication Data

Betenson, Lula Parker, 1884-
  Butch Cassidy, my brother.

  Bibliography: p. 259
  1. Cassidy, Butch, b. 1866 or 7. 2. Betenson, Lula
Parker, 1884-   I. Flack, Dora. II. Title.
F595.C362B47   364.1'55'0924 [B]   75-2332
ISBN 0-8425-1222-5

Library of Congress Catalog Card Number: 75-2332
International Standard Book Number: 0-8425-1222-5
Brigham Young University Press, Provo, Utah 84602
© 1975 Brigham Young University Press. All rights reserved
Third printing 1975
Printed in the United States of America
75 5M 16039

Contents and Illustrations

PICTURES

071644

MAPS, LETTERS, AND RECORDS

During the filming of *Butch Cassidy and the Sundance Kid,* **I visited the set in St. George, Utah. Paul Newman approached me and grinned, "Hi, I'm Butch." I replied, "Hi, I'm your sister."**

Foreword

When Butch and Sundance ran forward into the sunset, many hearts ran with them. Somehow they captured a piece of our past that was nostalgic. To us it was also synonymous with romance, free spirit, and the pure frontier sense of enterprise with a smile on its face. Technology has moved us all into a time zone of future shock and programmed behavior, of institutions and regimental controls. There seems to be a longing for the frontier space where one could freewheel a bit and where life was not quite so predictable.

Making the film was a pleasure—such a pleasure, in fact, I could be tempted to say that I felt guilty getting paid for it; but I'm not up to *that* kind of flight from reason. During the filming of *Butch Cassidy and the Sundance Kid,* I had the great enjoyment of meeting Lula Betenson, who exhibited a very convincing portrait of family traits, including a shrewd sensibility in dealing with the film company representatives.

Upon seeing the completed product, she said one thing that was both pleasing and original. She felt the picture had captured a quality long missed in the many glorified and historical accounts of the West and its characters—that rather than being a bunch of ruthless, psychotic, roaming killers, many of the "badmen" were, in fact, kids who never grew up or high spirited men whose sense of fun and pranks couldn't be contained by the law. This was the way we interpreted the legend in our film.

I am happy to say the friendship that has emerged between Lula and me has shown me that this free spirit still exists. Let us hope it will continue.

Robert Redford

Preface

For over forty years, sworn to silence, I have quietly listened to and read of the controversy about my brother, Butch Cassidy, and whether or not he and the Sundance Kid were killed in South America in 1909. Pinkerton's Detective Agency said he was, but many of his friends insisted they saw him in the United States long after the gun battle at San Vicente, Bolivia.

The members of the Wild Bunch have become legends that time has brightened rather than dimmed. My brother Butch in particular has emerged into a bigger-than-life image because of his winning personality—quite inconsistent with his brutal life. He was not a killer either by nature or reputation, but his friendly, singular charm and his interest in people—the struggling people—won for him their protection from the law. He was a rare composite of good and bad which has made him a dream-hero of young and old alike, and so the stories have expanded in number and imaginative detail.

Books written about him have been replete with errors borrowed back and forth from one author to another, mixed with the legends handed down by word of mouth, and embellished to spin a more sensational tale. But once the legend or half-truth appears in print, it is translated into absolute fact by the reader. The mistakes are compounded and are then generally considered irrefutable. One author makes a statement, true or false, without quoting his source; he, then, becomes the source for those who come after him. Few writers have documented specific details, and the reader is left to wonder where fact ends and fiction begins.

The stories became wilder and wilder. My brother was given credit for robberies which were committed at almost the same time, but many hundreds of miles apart, in the days of horseback travel. He would certainly have needed wings—and we know he was no angel.

Naturally I did not ride in the saddle behind him on his various escapades, so I cannot verify them. I include them only briefly, after having compared many sources, as what I conclude to be the closest to the truth, with an eye to chronology. Some of the many accounts placing him in widely separated areas at what would have to be the same time were straightened out for me by Butch himself, and many I am left to wonder about.

He was known as a Robin Hood in North and South America, robbing the rich and often giving to the poor. Of course, this does not alter the fact that he took things that didn't belong to him, and he took them by force. That I can never condone, no matter how generous he might have been with his spoils.

After one writer finished reading his far-out manuscript about Butch to me, I nodded my head and kept my silence. But now I have decided to tell the story as I know it. If I don't preserve my story in print, as only our family knew it, and not as others have frequently misquoted me, the facts will remain garbled and obscure. I regret that all my brothers and sisters are gone. They could have added so much to my account, especially my brothers who visited with him on his return.

The movie *Butch Cassidy and The Sundance Kid* has generated an extraordinary interest in my brother, and I am continually learning of new books being written about him. Actually, most of the episodes in the movie involved Elzy Lay instead of the Sundance Kid, but who would go to a movie entitled *Butch Cassidy and Elzy Lay*? This is only one example of how the facts can be distorted. The first part of the movie, however, is very typical of the boys. In my opinion, the stars presented an excellent portrayal. In fact, Paul Newman has a certain "family" look.

Because of the interest and questions generated by the movie and subsequent articles about my brother—most with distorted quotes from me—I have decided to break my sworn silence. I have no intention of making a "good boy" out of him, but if the story seems prejudiced, please remember that I am his sister. Because there was great love in our home, I find it impossible to be totally objective. However, I can honestly say that I have not found one person who knew him personally who will say a bad thing about him.

I must thank everyone who has helped me in any way to put this book together—you who knew my brother personally and you who knew of him. I am grateful for your concern and your cooperation.

The Quest
Chapter 1

I am the last survivor of Butch Cassidy's immediate family, ninety years of age as this book is written, in good health of mind and body. And I still have a question or two about life and circumstances—and especially about my brother, Robert LeRoy Parker. He was a child who, like Walt Whitman's child, went forth one day and became everything he saw.

My question is, what were the things he saw that led him to become an outlaw? Did he see too few roses and too many thorns? Too few rainbows and too many dark clouds? But if that were true, why wasn't he a bitter man, hated and despised, instead of loved and protected by those who knew him best?

I am intrigued that others have asked—and have attempted to answer—the same questions about him. Some people, unfamiliar with his background, assume that he came either from a broken home or from parents who mistreated or neglected him. Others point to the "bad company" he kept as a destructive influence in his life. I feel sure that some have labeled him inherently wild and uncontrollable, incapable of disciplining himself, so that he had no choice in the direction his life would take.

One of those people who have wondered about Butch's scorn for the law is Edward M. Kirby, principal of the Housatonic Valley Regional High School in Falls Village, Connecticut. In an attempt to bring alive the Old West for his students, he has spent several summers vaca-

1

My brother's gun. I have never ceased to wonder why he turned to it for a livelihood. I am thankful, though, that he never used this pistol, or any other gun, to take another's life. *Courtesy of Ron Lukas.*

tioning in the West and studying its history. I have received a letter from him containing some interesting observations about my brother. I believe the letter is representative of many who conjecture as to the reasons for Butch's waywardness.

> For the past several years I have been studying the life of Butch Cassidy and his Wild Bunch. . . . Wherever I have gone in Utah, Wyoming, and the rest of the Intermountain West, I have heard nothing but good things about Butch as a man. But the burning question in my mind remains: Why did the man Robert Leroy Parker become an outlaw? A man who in so many ways had so many positive things going for him? He was the first son of a fine, hard-working Mormon family. In pioneer times in Utah, he grew up imbued with the values of livestock, of land, and of living things. Why should a man such as this become an outlaw?
> We should first look at the period of time in which he grew up in a very wild part of these United States. He was a product of this massive land where man was many things but most of all was free. Freedom was most important to Butch as he traveled the outlaw trail from Canada to Mexico for many years. When he finished his active days on the outlaw trail, he traveled farther to South America and roamed the continent 3,000 miles from southern Argentina to Peru. Without question, Robert Leroy Parker was a man of the land, a man of the back country. If we analyze the life of Butch, comparing him to such outlaws as Jesse James, the Younger brothers, and Billy The Kid, we see the latter group as bitter products of social or personal conflict. Yet in the life of Butch Cassidy, we see none of this. The era of the mountain cowboy-outlaw stretches over but a short period of our history. Undoubtedly, such a man as Butch Cassidy realized subconsciously that he was part of an end of an era. Butch and his cohorts had three natural enemies which had encroached on the wild: the giant cattle companies, the banks, and the railroads. There doesn't seem to be much question that Butch saw these groups as threats to his way of life.

Robert Leroy Parker, with much more than average intelligence, gifted with organizational and leadership ability, could have been a great asset to 19th-century America. He might have been a congressman or a senator from his own state of Utah. A man of his caliber might have turned in any number of directions, but he chose outlawry. I make no excuses for this man. Above all, for people who knew him, he was a friend. A great friend, a man people could trust. His long existence in a most dangerous occupation must be attributed to the friends who protected him in both North and South America.

Perhaps the greatest rationale for the life that Butch Cassidy lived comes from the fact that he was a product of the great land, the big sky and the wide-open country. I would classify him as a libertarian, one who values his liberty above everything else and consciously or unconsciously fights to preserve it. Even today in southern Utah where Butch grew up, men struggle to save their land from giant industry and land developers. The citizens living there today must have a great resistance to becoming outlaws, but then perhaps they don't have the total libertarian desire of Butch Cassidy.

Robert Leroy Parker has become a living legend in the West as Butch Cassidy. He is not remembered so much for being an outlaw or for traveling far and wide on two continents as he is for being kind and loyal to the little guy, who was his real friend.

Edward M. Kirby
November 20, 1974

How much of what Kirby and others have speculated about Butch is true? I'd like to know. And maybe I can. That's the main reason I'm writing this book. Perhaps in setting down everything I have learned about him through my family, through reports of his activities, and from him directly, I can sift and sort through the facts and come up with some conclusions that will lay my questions to rest once and for all. It's about time; I'm not getting any younger.

I am the last link between the present generation and my grandparents, who were early Utah pioneers. I grew up listening to accounts of their lives as they related them to us. Since many writers begin Butch's story with his parentage and ancestry, I will do the same, hoping to set the record straight once and for all with the facts, as I know them. In the following chapters I will reveal for the first time intimate details about our family life and will discuss some of Butch's escapades—documenting from original sources where possible and from other printed sources where necessary—with the purpose of attempting to answer the question (for myself as well as for others) about the child Robert LeRoy Parker, who went forth and became Butch Cassidy, outlaw.

Parker Roots
Chapter 2

The cluster of men stood before the congregation in the log church in Beaver, Utah. Robert Parker, my paternal grandfather, held the new baby in his arms to give him a name and a blessing, according to Mormon custom. He proudly pronounced: "... And the name by which he shall be known on this earth and on the records of the Church is Robert LeRoy Parker...." Among others in the circle of men were my maternal grandfather, Robert Gillies, and Maximillian Parker, my father.

Our maternal grandparents, Robert and Jane Sinclair Gillies, lived in Beaver, but our paternal grandparents, Robert and Ann Hartley Parker, had traveled over eighty miles by horse and buggy from Washington, Utah, to be present on the important occasion of naming and blessing their first grandchild, my eldest brother, Robert, so named for both grandfathers.

None of the adoring adults who hovered over the baby that day in 1866 would have dreamed that their joy would some day change to heartache because of him. Robert LeRoy Parker was not the name by which he came to be known on the earth, for he assumed many aliases, the most common being Butch Cassidy.

So the child was born and began to go forth to see all that he would become.

Part of what he was to become, however—so psychologists tell us—was already rooted in his ancestry. If a part of the question about my brother can be answered

Our paternal grandfather, Robert Parker.

by knowing his ancestry better, let me tell what I know about it . Others who have done this have presented erroneous facts, and if in the process of revealing something about my brother I can also rectify these errors, I will feel rewarded.

Our grandparents, both the Parkers and the Gillies, and their families had known severe hardship and trouble as Mormon emigrant pioneers from England, but they were happy in their adopted homes in Utah Territory.

Grandfather and Grandmother Robert and Ann Hartley Parker[1] were both born in Burnley, Lancashire, England. According to my grandmother, Robert was an educated, handsome young man and an expert weaver by trade. And according to my grandfather, pretty Ann Hartley, who worked in the same textile mill, caught his eye.

In 1836 the first Mormon missionaries to England began preaching their new religion in the area, and grandfather Parker was convinced they had the true church. Ann was not a ready believer, but Robert and the missionaries finally convinced her of the truth of the gospel, much against her parents' wishes. After Ann's baptism, Grandfather and Grandmother were married in 1843 and moved to Accrington, Lancashire, where they continued to work in the textile mills.

A year later our father, Maximillian (Maxi),[2] was born. Four more children were born in Accrington: Martha Alice, Margaret, Arthur, and Emily.[3] Margaret and

---

1. Ann Hartley was born March 22, 1819. Records of The Church of Jesus Christ of Latter-day Saints, Genealogical Society, Salt Lake City, Utah.

Robert Parker was born March 29, 1820. Ibid. He was baptized November 7, 1840. Ibid.

Robert Parker and Ann Hartley were married May 25, 1843. Ibid.

2. Maximillian Parker was born June 8, 1844. Ibid.

3. Martha Alice was born on May 22, 1846; Margaret on May 8, 1848; Arthur on April 18, 1850; Emily on June 16, 1852.

Emily died in their first year. Then the family moved to Preston, where Ada was born.[4]

Leadership was natural to Grandfather Parker, and he was appointed Conference President[5] of the Church in Preston.

Grandmother was content caring for her small brood and their comfortable cottage with its vegetable garden and flowers. Life was good, and they were happy.

In America the main body of the Saints (as the Mormons called themselves) had been driven from their beautiful city of Nauvoo, Illinois, into Indian territory across the Mississippi River. They had crossed the Great Plains country to the Rocky Mountains and settled in the Valley of the Great Salt Lake. Brigham Young intended to make them a mighty people in the "tops of the mountains" and established settlements throughout the territory. He pleaded for tradesmen to leave the Old Country and help build the new Mormon empire. The Mormon missionaries who were spreading this cause in England often stayed at our grandparents' home. My father, Maxi's, duty was to polish their shoes, a task he detested.

Much to his distaste, Father was apprenticed at a very young age in the mill where Grandfather worked. One day he disgraced the family by running away from the mill. Grandfather, a stern disciplinarian, punished him severely, but Father remained adamant and refused to return to the mill—ever.

After lengthy deliberation, Grandfather decided the best course would be to go to America, as the mission-

4. Ada was born May 25, 1855, in Preston, Lancashire, England.

5. Journal History of The Church of Jesus Christ of Latter-day Saints.

10

aries urged. The Saints would need weavers in their desert outposts. His skill would be invaluable. This would give Maxi a chance to choose a livelihood more to his liking, he reasoned.

Grandmother was heartsick to leave the parents she dearly loved, in spite of their rejection of her faith. She realized too well that she would never see them again.

The cottage, the cow, and the furniture were all sold at a loss to raise the fare: nine pounds for persons over one year and four pounds and ten shillings for children under one year. Our father, Maxi, was eleven, Martha Alice nine, Arthur six, and baby Ada eight months. The sale netted them little more than boat passage, and they hoped they wouldn't need to borrow from the Perpetual Emigration Fund, a loaning institution set up to assist the emigrants, the money to be repaid when the emigrants were on their feet in the Valley.

The missionaries had been extolling the virtues of walking the more than thirteen hundred miles to Salt Lake, pushing belongings in a handcart. This would be a great adventure, they said. Grandfather was optimistic, but Grandmother knew it would be most difficult. With heavy heart she packed, knowing that a handcart wouldn't hold much for a family of six.

She couldn't leave her precious silverware nor her painting of *Juliet* which Grandfather had done when Maxi was born. Grandfather couldn't part with his painting *The Fisherman's Wife*. These would add color to their new home; so they were carefully packed on the bottom of the big trunk. In spite of limited space, Grandmother packed a good supply of clothing for her children.

On March 22, 1856,[6] Grandfather and Grandmother, with their children, boarded the ship *Enoch Train*

6. Journal History gives the date as March 22, 1856, but the list was published in the *Deseret News* as March 23. The McArthur Company had 100 handcarts, 5 wagons to carry extra supplies, 24 oxen, 4 mules, 25 tents, and provisions to last until they reached Florence, Nebraska. LeRoy R. and Ann W. Hafen, *Handcarts to Zion*, (Glendale, California: The Arthur H. Clark Co., 1960), p. 58.

Our paternal grandmother, Ann Hartley Parker.

and set sail for America. The company, headed by Daniel D. McArthur, a returning missionary, consisted of "534 souls." The sound of the bugle night and morning summoned them for prayers. Meetings were held at regular intervals. The Golden Rule was their motto, and, in spite of crowded conditions, the voyage could have been worse. They were on the water for five weeks, arriving at Boston on April 30. Four babies were born on board ship, and two individuals had died.

At New York City the group boarded a train, reaching the railroad terminal at Iowa City on May 12.

At Iowa City preparations were being made to outfit the first handcart companies. A month passed before they were ready to embark on their big experiment. Up to that time wagon trains had been the mode of conveyance, but Brigham Young had decided that handcarts would be quicker and easier. Former city dwellers from the Old World, he reasoned, would not have to learn how to handle teams. And the expense would be minimal. Brigham Young promised these pioneers that, as they walked, they would gain strength and resilience. He minimized the possible discomforts in an effort to move the people to the mountains at a faster rate.

The Ellsworth Company, the first handcart company, left Iowa City on June 9, 1856, with "274 souls."

Two days later the McArthur Company started out with 221 accounted for. Grandfather Robert Parker walked between the shafts of the handcart, leaning and pulling. Maxi, our father, who had just turned twelve, pushed. Martha Alice shepherded her six-year-old brother, Arthur, and Baby Ada rode on the handcart. The miles were made easier by everybody singing as they pushed and pulled:

> Ye Saints that dwell on Europe's shores,
> Prepare yourselves with many more

The Handcart Song

Pioneer Melody, arr.

14

To leave behind your native land
    For sure God's judgments are at hand.
Prepare to cross the stormy main
Before you do the valley gain
And with the faithful make a start
    To cross the plains with your hand cart.

CHORUS:
Some must push and some must pull
    As we go marching up the hill,
As merrily on the way we go
    Until we reach the valley, oh.

But ere before the valley gained
We will be met upon the plains
With music sweet and friends so dear
    And fresh supplies our hearts to cheer.
Then with the music and the song,
How cheerfully we'll march along
So thankfully you make a start
    To cross the plains with our hand carts.

(Repeat chorus)

When we get there amongst the rest
Industrious be and we'll be blessed,
And in our chambers be shut in
    While Judgment cleanse the earth from sin.
For well we know it will be so,
God's servants spoke it long ago,
And tell us it's high time to start
    To cross the plains with our hand carts.

(Repeat chorus)[7]

    Late in the afternoon of July 1, the company made camp. While Grandfather and Grandmother were

---

7. J. D. T. McAllister, "The Handcart Song" (The original song consisted of six verses), from *Handcarts to Zion* by LeRoy R. and Ann W. Hafen (Glendale, Calif.: The Arthur H. Clark Co., 1960), pp. 272-73.

busy with evening preparations, the children went off to play with other children of the company. A sudden quick rainstorm sent them scurrying to their parents, but the shower passed almost immediately. Grandmother Ann continued her supper routine, then called the children to eat.

"Where's Arthur?" she asked. Her youngsters shook their heads. She inquired of others who had been playing with them, but no one had seen him. She called and searched in vain. Everyone else joined the hunt, which continued all night and into the next day. Still no Arthur.

The company could not be delayed indefinitely. Elder McArthur reluctantly insisted they must move on.

"You go with the company, Ann," Grandfather said. "I'll retrace the backtrail and find the boy. Then I'll catch up with you. Now don't worry—I'll find him."

Grandmother took a red shawl from the handcart and put it over Grandfather's arm. "If you find him, wave this in the distance, and I'll know he's all right. Wrap him in it if you find him—" She couldn't bring herself to say the word. She watched his figure fade into the landscape, then turned her face westward. Slipping under the crosspiece of the handcart, she started to pull. Maxi pushed harder than ever.

For the sake of the children, she tried to hide her despair. When night came, she was so weary she couldn't sleep. Instead she cried and prayed, wondering if Arthur and her husband had been killed by Indians or wild animals. The company, silently sharing her grief, traveled slower to give Robert a chance to catch up.

July 3 and 4 passed the same way. Each evening she climbed to the highest spot and peered anxiously into the distance until dark. Traveling at the end of the company to keep an eye on the backtrail, Grandmother Ann and her children were caked with dust.

After camp was made on the night of the 4th, Grandmother walked a short distance to a little clump of trees. Exhausted and heartbroken, she sank to her knees. After this long time, there was little hope of their return. She cried, "Dear Lord, if I've done wrong to come, if I've lost my dear husband and my little son, thy will be done.

But if they return, I'll never question again. I am in thy keeping."

Another back-breaking, blinding day followed. The blistering summer sun beat down mercilessly. The company broke for camp early that evening. She walked up on a little hill and peered out across the country. Was that a moving object in the distance? She blinked her eyes to clear her vision. The moving spot dropped out of sight. Her heart sank and she knelt down under a small tree, praying fervently.

As she started back toward camp, she turned for one last look. There it was again! An object moved up over a little rise. Was it? Yes, it looked like a man. The sun was behind a cloud, and she couldn't see too well. As the man moved closer, by his walk she knew he was Grandfather. A gasp of joy escaped her lips, then smothered in her throat. He walked alone! She froze in her tracks. At that instant the sun came out, and she caught a glimpse of red in the sun's rays.

Grandmother screamed the good news to the camp and ran to meet her lost ones. Gathering her son in her arms, her weariness gone, she carried Arthur to camp in order to relieve her exhausted, gaunt husband.[8]

Grandfather related his experience to the rejoicing camp. "On my second night of searching, I stumbled into a trading post, where I learned that a man and his wife who lived some distance away had found Arthur, lost, frightened and very hungry. I rested only a few hours. Then carrying a little food with me, I followed directions to their cabin and found Arthur. Arthur told me how the big dogs stood around him that first night and barked, but they didn't touch him." Grandfather swallowed hard. "Of course, the dogs were wolves. But he'd been protected by all our prayers. I walked almost continuously day and night to catch you, carrying little Arthur most of the time—poor tired little tyke."

8. Hafen, *Handcarts to Zion*, pp. 63-64.

That was the first night's rest in five nights for Grandfather and Grandmother. Next morning Grandfather couldn't get to his feet; so Grandmother begged a ride for him in one of the supply wagons.

Sundays were always a pleasant relief. On that day clothes were washed and dried, services were held, and everyone rested, reviving bodies and spirits.

When the company reached Florence, two weeks were spent repairing handcarts, getting fresh supplies of food and other necessities, washing, and preparing for the thousand-mile trek yet ahead of them. Since Grandfather's health didn't improve much, Grandmother and Maxi, my father, continued to pull the load.

Fort Laramie meant another rest stop and repairs. The diet by that time had become monotonous—usually hard biscuits or corn bread cooked over an open fire and salt pork.

Grandmother unwrapped her beautiful silverware—her last precious possession. She and Father walked into the Fort to trade her silver in order to replenish her food supply. She bought fresh apples, one for Grandfather and one for each of the children, and a bit of candy. Never were apples so juicy and candy so sweet.

The Ellsworth Company had preceded the McArthur Company into the Great Salt Lake Valley by two days; so Brigham Young sent wagons to meet the new arrivals as they trudged down the rough mountain trail. When they caught their first glimpse of the Valley spread before them, a shout of joy rang out. Caps flew into the air.

The few remaining possessions of the group were transferred to the wagons, and there was room enough for everyone to ride. Just before climbing into the wagon, Grandmother said, "I've had enough!" She gave the rickety old handcart a shove over the rim of the canyon and didn't feel a tinge of remorse as she heard it breaking up on the rocks below. They arrived in the Valley on September 26, 1856, after three and a half long, hot months of pushing and pulling. Only seven persons in their company died during the trek.

The Parker family stayed in Great Salt Lake City until the fall, then moved to American Fork, about twenty-five miles to the south, where Grandfather taught school. However, because of his skill as a weaver, he was soon called to Beaver to help with the woolen mill there.

Winter was too close for Grandfather to build another cabin, and the family was forced to live in a dug-out—a cave dug back into an earth bank with a roof of poles and dirt pounded hard. Shortly after they moved in, the fall storms began. Rain sent water trickling down the walls and streaming through the ceiling. Muddy water collected on the earthen floor, making the dugout damp, musty, and cold all winter.

The following summer, Grandfather, with Father's help, built a one-room cabin with a puncheon floor and a snug roof. The family was crowded but comfy. Two more rooms were added the following spring.

Father, at age eighteen, made two trips to St. Louis, Missouri, bringing converts west for the Perpetual Emigration program. Although he wasn't paid for these trips, he worked in St. Louis while waiting, and made a little money. With his earnings he bought presents for the family, cooking kettles for his mother, and other household items she couldn't buy in the west. For himself, he bought a pair of fancy dancing pumps because he loved to dance. Three more Parker children were born in Beaver: Robert, who died as a baby, Ellen, and Ruth Caroline.[9]

Because of nearly losing Arthur during the westward trek, Grandmother always favored the boy. When he was about seventeen, he and a Skinner boy decided to go

9. Robert was born January 12, 1858, and died in 1859. Ellen was born February 12, 1860. Ruth Caroline was born April 5, 1862—all in Beaver, Utah.

Information about the Parker children was taken from family records belonging to Ruth S. Stringham, Salt Lake City, Utah.

to California to find work. No amount of reasoning could bend his will. The two boys made up an outfit and started out. They were never heard from. Part of their wagon was discovered, and the families presumed they had been killed by Indians. Grandmother waited and watched for his return for years, to no avail.

The woolen mill in Beaver prospered. But now the church leaders wanted to set up a cotton and silk mill in southern Utah. Brigham Young was eager that the Saints should be self-sustaining; so he sent out instructions for raising cotton and silkworms for cloth production. The climate in Utah's Dixie in the St. George area was warm enough for cotton, and the Virgin River was dammed to provide water. Brigham Young's emissaries taught the people throughout the settlements how to raise mulberry trees, and silkworms were imported from China. Grandfather was among those called to work in the weaving mill at Washington, Utah. He and Grandmother spent the rest of their lives there.

When the railroad was completed, cloth could be imported cheaper than it could be manufactured locally. Grandfather was without a job; so he took over the management of the local co-op store, which was in the red. He carried everything from nails to hand-painted china. In a short time he had the store paying dividends. He also managed the post office which was housed in the same building. In the early days of Washington only one copy of the Deseret News came to town. Most of the townspeople congregated at the post office and listened to Grandfather read the news to them out of the paper.

In his later years Grandfather returned to England on a mission for the Church. All his life he was a faithful church member. He was an excellent speaker, and he led the choir. He could whistle like a bird and entertained people freely with his talent. He'd do anything for the Church and was more staunch than his descendants. Always well-groomed, he carried himself with pride and was stern but kind.

Loved for her kindness, Grandmother was an excellent homemaker. Her rose garden and white picket-fenced yard looked like an old-fashioned picture. Eventually Grandfather built a house on the store lot.

I still have Grandfather Robert Parker's little account book, a small leather-bound book about 3" x 5". Its pages are filled with miscellaneous entries in his own careful handwriting: figures of accounts, names and addresses and dates of people who were in his "conference" back in England, lists of tithing payments entered in shillings and pence. There are even poems, which I presume he wrote himself. Surprisingly, there is a marked similarity between his handwriting and my brother Robert LeRoy Parker's.

During the past years, so-called historians have recorded a maudlin story about Grandfather Robert Parker dying on the plains in the early winter snows which beset the Martin Handcart Company. Of course, as I have previously explained and documented, the Parkers came in the second company during the summer months with the McArthur Company, not with the Martin Company. This is a perfect example of a mistake borrowed from one author to another until it is thought to be absolute fact.

I visited my grandparents Parker many times and lived with them for over six months as a young girl and can remember their telling the events that have been related here. They are both buried in the Washington Cemetery and inscribed tombstones over their graves read as follows:

Robert Parker	Ann Parker
born Mar. 29, 1820	born
in Burnley	Mar. 22, 1819
Lancashire, Eng.	in Lancashire, Eng.
died	died
Feb. 24, 1901	Jan. 25, 1899
St. George, Utah	Washington, Utah

Tombstone of Robert and Ann Parker in Washington, Utah, cemetery. *Courtesy of A. LeGrand Flack.*

Of his Parker grandparents' traits: leadership ability, dedication to a cause to the point of deprivation, hardiness and perseverance, sternness with kindness, an enterprising zeal, and an abiding love for family and for God, I do know that my brother inherited at least a portion. It is natural, I suppose, for a family's recounting of ancestral history to be somewhat biased. Perhaps I have left out something significant. I am thinking that Grandmother Parker's pushing her handcart off a cliff to signify her liberation from that kind of hardship could have been a beginning to the free spirit my brother Butch evidenced when he embarked on the life of an outlaw.

But the Parkers are only a part of his ancestry; the Gillies must also be taken into account.

Robert and Jane Gillies
Chapter 3

My mother was Annie Campbell Gillies, the eldest daughter of Robert and Jane Sinclair Gillies, a Scottish couple who joined the Mormon church in England. All my life I grew up thinking that the Gillies family came to the Salt Lake Valley in the Edward Martin Handcart Company, the ill-fated last company of 1856.[1]

However, a search of the emigration records of The Church of Jesus Christ of Latter-day Saints reveals that the Gillies family was included with the William B. Hodgett wagon train, which traveled closely with the Martin Handcart Company and at times camped alongside them. The two groups were later snowed in together when early storms and frigid temperatures made progress impossible. Consequently, Mother would have known many of the events which occurred in the handcart company and would have had many of the same experiences. The wagons of any train were so heavily loaded that able-bodied persons walked the whole distance. My mother did. I am sure that this is why I always thought she came with the Martin Handcart Company.

---

1. Only ten handcart companies came to the Valley, five of them in 1856, two in 1857, one in 1859, and two in 1860. A total of 2,962 persons traveled in these companies and only about 250 deaths occurred en route. LeRoy R. and Ann W. Hafen, *Handcarts to Zion* (Glendale, California: The Arthur H. Clark Co., 1960), p. 193.

Our maternal grandfather, Robert Gillies.

Mother was nine years old when her family left Liverpool, England—their destination Great Salt Lake Valley. Other children in the family were an older brother Moroni, a younger brother Daniel, and a little sister Christina.[2]

On May 25, 1856, a large company of 856 Saints watched from the deck of the ship *Horizon* as England faded into the distance. The passengers took care of their own crowded quarters and did their own cooking. One day Robert Gillies (my grandfather) was draining the water off boiled potatoes when a sudden breeze lifted his hat. It was either lose the potatoes or his hat. He saved the food and watched his hat fly away in the wind.

After a favorable voyage of six weeks, they landed at New York City and went by train to Iowa City by way of Albany, Buffalo, and Chicago, reaching Iowa City on July 7.[3]

So eager to reach "Zion" were these travelers that the last groups to sail from England in that year were much larger than anticipated. Trouble arranging for passage had delayed them. When they arrived at Iowa City, sufficient wagons and handcarts were not available. Not having the means to stay in Iowa City the entire winter, the emigrants called a consultation meeting, wherein they were warned of the dangers of starting out so late in the season; winter storms would surely beset them. But they were determined to go on, feeling that the Lord would temper the elements to accommodate them. Hastily they threw together handcarts constructed of green wood. Con-

2. The Gillies family was listed in Emigration records as follows (the number gives the age of each individual):

Gillies, Robert (36) from Scotland
   Jane (35)
   Moroni (10)
   Ann (9) [Her name is really Annie]
   Daniel (7)
   Christian (3) [This is actually a girl named Christina]

3. Hafen, *Handcarts to Zion*, pp. 91, 193.

Our maternal grandmother, Jane Sinclair Gillies.

sequently, as the wood dried, necessary repair and replacement problems slowed the journey.

Three handcart companies were already en route to the Valley. The Fourth Handcart Company under Capt. James G. Willie left Iowa City on July 15, 1856. Capt. Hodgett's thirty-three-wagon company with 185 passengers followed a few days later. The Gillies family was in this company. Thirteen days later, on July 28, the Fifth Handcart Company under Capt. Edward Martin left for Salt Lake Valley.[4]

Indians were a constant danger. Mother told of seeing the long blond hair of a white woman wrapped around the wheel hub of a wagon that had been partly burned by Indians. What a terrifying thing for anyone to see, especially for children.

Handcarts moved faster than ox trains, and the Martin group soon caught up with Hodgett's wagon train. Contrary to expectations, winter storms blew in earlier than usual. The ground was frozen too hard to dig graves to bury the dead. On November 6 the thermometer dropped to ten degrees below zero at Devil's Gate. Rescue wagons had been sent out from Salt Lake City, but they, too, were stopped in the deep snow.

Hodgett's and Hunt's wagon trains were both halted at Devil's Gate along with the Martin Handcart Company. In such severe cold, handcart travel was impossible. The sick handcart members were put in the wagons, and most of the deteriorated handcarts were abandoned. In this way the travelers hoped to reach the Valley. The food supply had been exhausted for some time; each person was rationed to less than a half pound of flour per day. Because of the difficult privations, some of the handcart people temporarily lost their senses. Almost one hundred and fifty of the original five hundred and seventy-six emigrants lost their lives on the trek.

Rescue wagons found the floundering emigrants at Devil's Slide and distributed welcome food, supplies,

4. Hafen, *Handcarts to Zion*, p. 193.

and clothing. With this relief and a break in the bitter weather, they continued on, reaching the Salt Lake Valley on November 30.

Some of the travelers lost limbs due to freezing, but the Gillies family suffered no lasting ill effects from the journey. They settled in Woods Cross, north of Salt Lake City, Utah, where they lived for some time. Grandfather Gillies was a skilled carpenter and cabinetmaker, and he and his family were called to settle in Beaver. I still have a table made by Grandfather Gillies in my home.

A few years after moving to Beaver, Grandfather Gillies made a business trip back to Woods Cross, where he died of pneumonia on October 6, 1866, at the age of forty-six—six months after the birth of his first grandson, Robert LeRoy Parker.[5]

My grandmother, Jane Sinclair Gillies, was a peppery little Scotswoman with the determination to gather her family close and make a good life. Always active in church affairs, she served as a teacher and a leader. She was a typical thrifty Scotswoman. My father, her son-in-law, often said that Grandmother Gillies could stretch a gallon of milk a day to keep her family in milk and butter—and sell some to boot. Her sense of humor was refreshing, but her tongue was sharp; believe me, we listened when she spoke. Grandmother Gillies lived to be eighty-four years old.

The Gillies' legacy of personal traits, then, compares in significant ways with that of the Parkers. Their championing of an unpopular religion to the point of nearly relinquishing their lives, their hardiness in the face of difficulties, their love for their family—these are characteristics hardly to be thought of as contributing to waywardness in a descendant. I wonder, though, if my brother Bob ever chafed at Grandmother Gillies's thriftiness and her caustic tongue? Could these have been a beginning to his opposition to restrictions, or did that kind of resentment come later?

5. Family records in possession of Una Gillies, Green River, Utah.

The Child
Robert LeRoy
Parker
Chapter 4

When my grandparents Gillies and their family moved to Beaver, Utah, from Woods Cross in the 1860s, the eldest daughter Annie (my mother) was a pretty, charming lass. Before long she caught the eye of Maximillian Parker (my father). In those days "home grown" entertainment, in the form of plays and programs, was about the only social diversion. Annie and Max were usually cast in the plays. Max was quite a comedian, a trait which was to show up in my generation. Annie always had a song on her lips and was very sociable.

When Father's parents, Robert and Ann Parker, were called in 1865 to help in the new cotton mill in Washington, Utah, my father stayed behind in Beaver. He had eyes only for Annie and wasn't about to take chances on losing her.

Father and Mother were married on Annie's birthday, July 12, 1865.[1]

In the early years of their marriage Father carried the mail on horseback from Beaver to Sanford Bench (later Panguitch, Utah) on the Sevier River. The Indians were a constant source of trouble. Often at some sign of lurking danger, as Father loped along on his horse, the hair on his head almost raised his hat. Was that birdcall an

---

1. LDS Church records and family records.

Indian imitation? At times he had what he thought was a premonition that an Indian arrow would knock him from his horse.

Mother worried endlessly about her young husband, but he completed his years of service without Indian interference. Later he fought in the Black Hawk war, for which he earned a small pension. Still later, veterans' reunions were an eagerly anticipated annual event for him.

Ironically, Annie's and Max's first son, Robert LeRoy Parker, my brother, was born on Friday, April 13, 1866, in Beaver, Utah.[2]

As Father rode his horse back and forth to Sanford Bench on his mail route, he became more and more impressed that Circle Valley, along the Sevier River, would be a fine place to raise his family. He liked the looks of it. After considerable scouting he found a promising spot three miles south of the town of Circleville in the mouth of Circleville Canyon, surrounded by mountains, with the river close by.

He consulted with Mother, who was reluctant to leave Beaver; but at last she said, "If you think it's best, Max, I'll go along." Father bought the place from a man

---

2. Family records were kept by my father, Maximillian, of dates and events concerning his family. His book gives April 13 as the date instead of April 6, which is generally printed.

No birth certificates are available in Utah for this early period. LDS ward records are the only official information source. Apparently they were not preserved that early in the Beaver area because there are no records of the eldest children in our family. The younger children are all recorded as they should be. The 1880 Census of Circle Valley lists the family of Maximillian Parker and Annie Gillies Parker. Robert L., age fourteen, is the eldest child. This, then, becomes the only independent official proof that his name was Robert instead of George, as other records and writers have recorded.

by the name of James and moved his family. There was a two-room cabin at the foot of a hill. This became home for our family and is still standing as the Butch Cassidy Home.

When several families had attempted to settle the town of Circleville a few years before, the Indians drove them out. Later settlers found insurmountable difficulties. The first year Father planted wheat, he repeated the sowing three times. First, the wind blew it right out of the ground. Then, as the seed germinated after the second planting, the wind whipped off the new sprouts. However, he did harvest the third planting.

Canals had to be dug to get water to the land. This took time. In town a small log schoolhouse was built, and it doubled as a church. The two stores in Circleville were owned by John Fullmer and Laban Morrill. James Whittaker owned the first saloon on his ranch north of town. He also owned a gristmill in nearby Kingston, where residents took their grain to be ground into flour. There was always a mudhole in front of Whittaker's saloon on the highway where the wagons were invariably bogged down. The drivers, exasperated over being stuck in the mud, would go into the saloon for refreshment. If they thought they were loaded when they went in, they were really "loaded" when they came out.

Several stalwart families moved from Beaver to Circleville: the Daltons (not the outlaws), the Wileys, and the Thompsons. So Father and Mother were not among strangers. By this time the family had expanded to six children. Bob, the eldest, thirteen years old, was Father's right-hand man. The older children attended school in Beaver. Some of the teachers were Richard Horne, R. T. Thurber, O. U. Bean, William Johnson, Vie Christen, May Smith, and Charley Stoney. Bob had hired out to Pat Ryan, who lived in the area, and Pat reported that Bob could do a man's work and was completely dependable.

The log house already on the Parker Ranch in Circle Valley had a large room with a fireplace. This room served as a combination kitchen and living room, and a small room was the bedroom. According to the prevailing custom, Mother covered the ceiling with large pieces of "factory," a cheap white cloth which gave the room a more liveable appearance and blocked out the crude roof beams. The rough floor was covered with homemade rag carpets stretched over straw for padding. Every year fresh straw was laid, and the carpets were cleaned outside, then tacked back in place. We filled bed ticks with cornhusks or straw. Lace curtains, stiffly starched, hung at the windows. As soon as possible, Dad built on a large room to the east which became the kitchen and two rooms on the south as much-needed bedrooms. The granary, sheds, and corrals were all to the north of the house.

The brush had to be cleared from the land to make it a profitable farming operation. Since this took much time and hard work, there wasn't enough money to make ends meet. Dad got work at Frisco, a mining town west of Beaver, cutting ties for the railroad and studding for the mines. He traveled back and forth between Frisco and the ranch, according to the work available, and he freighted and hauled timber for charcoal. As a result, progress on our land was very slow. The boys were good workers and all helped Mother, but they needed Dad. Of course, since Bob was the eldest, he took the heaviest work load.

That first winter in Circle Valley (1879-80) was perhaps the most severe recorded. The extreme cold wiped out our herd of cattle except for two cows, named Hutch and Sal. The family didn't recover financially from this setback for years.

My parents homesteaded additional property, but the land was jumped. Dad was furious. In those days, disagreements were heard by the bishop who, in the absence of the civil law, acted as a judge in a bishop's court. Dad lost the land. He was so hurt, he would have left the church if it hadn't been for Mother.

Even though life for the Parkers was a struggle, it was not all work and no play. Our parents' love of fun was passed on to us children. Every evening was "home evening." Being isolated on the ranch, we of course had to make our own good times. Our parents sang a lot and told stories of the things they used to do. Repetition of these

Parker Ranch: cabin in the trees; granary and corrals in right of picture. *Courtesy of Parker Hamilton, Flagstaff, Arizona.*

stories imprinted them indelibly on our minds. The children all had good singing voices, and we enjoyed the bond of music. Bob played the harmonica. My older brothers and sisters often reminisced about these incidents and memories.

Bob adored Mother. When he was in a frolicsome mood, he waltzed her around the room, then picked her up bodily and set her on the table. "Come on, kids," he announced, "Bring the crown. Ma's the queen."

"LeRoy! Put me down!" she would protest. (Mother and Dad always called him LeRoy, but the kids called him Bob.)

Bob was always up to some outlandish devilment. At the height of the summer when the grasshoppers had achieved full growth, he called, "Arthur, help me catch some of these critters." (My brother Arthur had been named for Uncle Arthur, who had been lost on the plains and who later disappeared on his way to California.)

"Ah, why you wanta catch grasshoppers?" Arthur asked.

"You'll see," Bob grinned mischievously. In a few minutes they had captured some whoppers.

"Now what?" Arthur asked.

"Run and get some string from Ma," Bob instructed. Running pell-mell, Arthur soon returned with the string. A master with knots, Bob skillfully secured long strings to the grasshoppers' legs. "The finish line for our race is the edge of Ma's flower bed. These hoppers are our prize racehorses. I'll beat ya! On your mark, get set, go!" Bob yelled. He had seen to it that his little brother Arthur had the biggest hopper. The two guided their "racehorses" to the finish lines.

"I beat!" Arthur shrieked jubilantly.

The rest of the kids took turns for a real race riot. On another day, they pretended the captive hoppers were workhorses; but always it was fun for everyone.

The boys (with Bob's encouragement) sometimes staged a make-believe rodeo by riding the calves. In their imaginations, they were hard-riding broncobusters.

This was Bob's early training. He graduated to horses very early in life. He seldom had trouble breaking a horse, for he understood and loved animals. Our animals were all named. One cow, with big brown eyes, was called Sarah, after one of the town ladies.

Bob kept a friendly magpie around the place, which he had trained to talk. The bird could say, "Hello, hello!" or something simple like that. Bob made a birdcage out of slender willow strips in which he kept his magpies. The cage stayed in the family for many, many years. The boys always had pets. There was once a goat which they hitched to a homemade cart. There were rabbits, pigeons, and chipmunks, each one named.

Bob made a fuss over kids, and they loved him, whether they were our own, our relatives', or neighbors'. There was always room on his horse for as many as could scramble up. If they were little, he'd put them all on and lead the horse.

Bob built a raft, crowded on it every kid he could, and took them for a ride on the nearby pond. This was great sport, and he enjoyed it more than any of his young passengers.

One day Dad spotted Bob's rear end protruding from under the granary. "LeRoy," he called, as he sauntered over. "What are you doing under the granary?" For a moment the prone figure froze. "Come on out," Dad ordered.

Bob wiggled out backward and brushed the dust from his clothes. "I—I was just lookin' for a skunk," he muttered.

"That's a dangerous animal to go after. If you found him, we'd have to bury you for sure," Dad joshed. He turned to walk away, then sniffed suspiciously. "Sure that was a skunk you were after?"

Bob hung his head. He didn't have to admit he'd been tampering with tobacco he had hidden there. Dad waggled his finger at Bob. "That's not much better'n a skunk. Your mother will be upset. No more, you understand? You're apt to burn down the granary."

How could Dad ever foresee the fate of that granary? But in good conscience he couldn't pursue the lecture, because he did a little smoking himself. He remembered how he and other town boys had burned wood in the "bottoms" for lye, but the boys had also taught him to smoke bark, and that had been the beginning.

Dad might have been termed a "jack Mormon," and the boys, for the most part, followed his example. But Mother was a faithful churchgoer. And even when Dad was not there to help her she saw to it that we went to our meetings. We were never forced to go, however, and Bob wasn't a willing attender. If he could find some chore—any chore—that needed his attention, he stayed home to take care of it. Any excuse was convenient.

When Bob was about ten, Mother dressed him up in new trousers to go to the weekly religion class. He walked off reluctantly down the road. Mother watched. Bob obviously thought he had given her enough time to go into the house, for he was some distance away. She saw him suddenly drop to the ground and roll in the dust, just like a horse. He didn't come home for a long while. When he finally returned, she asked, "Where did you pick up all that dirt, young man?"

"Well, a bull chased me."

"Oh?" she intoned knowingly. "Why have you been gone so long? Seems like you'd have made it home a lot quicker if a bull was after you."

"Well, the bull just stood there in front of me and pawed the dirt, and I didn't dare move."

"I'm glad that bull didn't catch you," she observed, knowing full well there was no reason to get excited. But she didn't insist that he go again if he made a fuss.

During one of her thirteen confinements, Mother was in Beaver so that Grandma Gillies could help with the new baby. My eldest sister tried to take care of things at the ranch while Mother was gone. Mother knew that with the help of the boys Sister could manage.

One day during Mother's absence, Sister decided to make a pair of pants for my brother Eb, going on five. She wasn't an expert seamstress, but after a struggle she proudly put her handiwork on Eb and scooted him outside to play. When he came into the house, she was perplexed; the new pants were split out already. She kept sewing them up, but every time he came in, he was out of them.

Just then Jim Kittleman knocked on the door. He was a kind old neighbor of ours, a bachelor, and his property was about half a mile north of us. Mother was always very good to Mr. Kittleman, taking him fresh bread and other goodies. On that particular day, Jim came over to see how the Parkers were getting along without Mother. He noticed that Eb's pants looked rather strange. On closer examination he threw back his head and laughed. Sister looked at him, feeling a little hurt. "What's the matter, Mr. Kittleman?"

Mr. Kittleman wiped the tears from his eyes and stripped off Eb's split pants. He held them up so she could see what he meant, as he explained. "Lookee here, girl. You got the legs part sewed up for the waist part. Ya see, the legs of trousers are cut skinnier than the part around the belly. There's no room for the little tyke to move, with 'em sewed up this way. That's why they're all split out."

Sister was embarrassed. "Oh, thank you, Mr. Kittleman. I couldn't imagine what was the trouble." She picked them apart and sewed them up properly, and Eb was comfortable in his new pants.

Mr. Kittleman's weakness was wine. He bought it in kegs and imbibed freely until a keg was empty. Oh, he had plenty of help from bums that sponged off him. At one time his sister Pinkie came and lived with him for a while. She was such a nice person, but she couldn't take that drinking and didn't stay long.

One day the Parker youngsters got hold of some of Mr. Kittleman's wine when Mother had gone to town. They poured it in pans for the chickens. When Mother returned, all the chickens were reeling and crowing and acting very strange. She looked at those tumbling chickens, puzzled. She couldn't imagine what was wrong and wondered if they would have to be destroyed. Did they have some rare malady? When she smelled the boys' breath, she knew what was wrong with them. But she didn't know what to do with those wobbling chickens. However, apparently it didn't hurt them, for they seemed perfectly sober and normal the next day, with no evidence of a hangover.

As the family grew in size and number, money continued to be scarce for the family's needs. Bob worked wherever he could get a job when he wasn't needed at home. Mother felt she should be doing more to help out financially. She decided that during the summers she would move to the Marshall Ranch, twelve miles south of Circleville, where she could dairy and bring in a little extra money. Dad didn't want this, but she reasoned that with three husky boys to help her, their labors would go a long way toward putting them on their feet. By this time there were four boys and three girls in the family. So, during the summer, Mother ran a dairy, making butter and cheese to sell.

The Marshall Ranch was a large open spread, surrounded by mountains, similar to Circle Valley. There was plenty of open land for grass, with water on it. The ranch house was situated on the west, not far from the hilly boundary. The small house where we lived and dairied was a little farther west of the big ranch house. It is no longer there. From the vantage point of the houses, one could keep an eye on the cattle for miles to the north, south and east, with hills to the west.

By the second season at the Marshall Ranch, Mike Cassidy had drifted into the country. He was sort of a shady character, and he fell in with a couple of fellows in the valley who weren't too honest—Fred and Charley. It became known later that Mike was an outlaw. Mike worked around that part of the country wherever he could get a job. It was soon evident that he knew all the tricks of cattle- and horse-stealing, and he used them.

In those days, much of the western United States was occupied by so-called cattle barons whose vast herds roamed the territory. This was public land. The

40

transcontinental railroad was completed at Promontory, Utah, in 1869; so the big cattlemen had herds on the move much of the time, driving them to the few western railroad centers. Of course, small ranchers or homesteaders tried to claim a rightful share of the public land. But the powerful cattlemen resented this, and life was difficult for the little man, who regarded the big operators as range hogs. Grabbing strays from the big herds was the just spoils of war, the little man reasoned. How could anyone who had thousands of head of cattle miss a few here and there as they grazed unwatched on an area covering hundreds of miles?

Consequently, young men took vengeance by rounding up and branding mavericks with their own marks. All the big outfits did the same, and it was hard to draw the line between mavericking and rustling. It was like the pot calling the kettle black. Naturally, these common practices added up to trouble, leading men over that thin line into the real world of stealing, with all its compounded woes. One thing led to another to the point of no return. The cowboys took bigger and bigger chances until one day, often without their realizing that it was happening, they found themselves outlaws.

Although Mother was quite naive, she knew something questionable was going on out there in the corral at the Marshall Ranch. She wasn't blind. But others worked for Marshall; so it was beyond her control. Her responsibility ended at the dairy barn. She questioned Bob. "What's going on out there in the corral?"

"Oh, nothing," he assured her. "They're just branding cattle."

However, Mother's apprehension grew with the attention and favors Mike showered on Bob, but she seemed helpless to alter the situation. Bob admired Mike openly and was eager to learn all his skills with horses and cattle. Mike really knew how to handle animals. Then Mike gave Bob a gun and trained him in its use. He also gave him a saddle for his horse.

Mother felt if she interfered too much, she might turn her son away, and she wanted to hold him more than ever. So she moved the family back to the ranch in Circle Valley. Bob was a grown young man now. He had been dependable in spite of his craving for excitement. Surely she could depend on him to make the right choices. Or could she? She knew Mike was mixed up with Fred and Charley, and she didn't trust that pair, either.

She sensed that Bob was growing restless, not without reason. He'd seen little but hard work, day in and day out, and not much pay. To a young man, this sort of life didn't hold much promise. In spite of the struggle, though, she thought, when you had your family and there was love, it was worth it. And things would improve in time, Mother assured herself.

I was born April 5, 1884, just before Mother moved from the Marshall Ranch back to Circle Valley. Bob turned eighteen the week after I was born. Mother noticed he seemed moody and preoccupied, not his old rambunctious self. She couldn't break down his reserve.

At our ranch one June afternoon, Mother stood at the open door drinking in the late afternoon sunshine. Her troubled spirits lifted as she gazed at the five poplar trees in the yard, west of the house. Those trees seemed to give her assurance. She had watched them grow from saplings, and they were flourishing. She and LeRoy had brought them from Beaver and planted them. In the distance, she could see the children trooping home from the river where they'd enjoyed a light picnic. She turned back to the cookstove, polished to a shining black. From the oven she lifted a big, black, square dripper-pan filled with tempting loaves of bread. She turned them onto the table to cool and glanced out the door as she heard faint hoofbeats in the distance. Could that be her firstborn?

Shortly Bob's lean frame filled the doorway. He grinned at her as he hung his jacket on the nail inside and put his hat over it. Looking into his hazel eyes, Mother knew something was wrong. When things were right, he

Butch helped Mother plant these poplar trees on our ranch. *Courtesy of Parker Hamilton, Flagstaff, Arizona.*

was full of fun—chuckling and teasing—and he always gave his hat a twirl from the doorway and sent it sailing for a chair post or some other jutting object—invariably hitting its mark. The younger children were just then trailing leisurely into the yard from their outing.

"What is it, LeRoy?" Mother asked.

"Ummm, nothing smells as good as your bread, Ma," he replied, avoiding her question. "Do I have to wait for supper?"

"No," she chuckled. She cut him a thick piece of the steaming bread and spread it generously with home-made butter and bullberry preserves.

"Umm, my favorite. Nothing like bullberry p'serves." He barely finished the slice before the children burst into the kitchen. Immediately they were all over him, the small ones hugging his legs, the bigger ones tousling his hair or punching his muscles, testing them for hardness.

This was no time or place for serious conversation. But after the young ones were settled down for the night and the older ones were outside with chores, again Mother tried to cut through Bob's reserve. He'd been especially tender with the little ones as he kissed them good night. He sauntered to the cradle and pulled back the blanket snuggled around the new baby. He tweeked the pink cheek and winked at Mother. "Cute, huh?"

"That's the word for her, if ever there was one," she chuckled. "She missed being your eighteenth birthday present by eight days; that puts Lula real close to you." (Although I was far too young to know what was happening, Mother often recounted the details of this memorable day. And, believe it or not, my family nickname was always *Cute*, even if it wasn't apropos. All of us children had nicknames.)

"LeRoy—what's eating you?"

He tried to shrug it off, but could see that he wasn't very convincing. "I'm leaving bright and early in the morning."

"Leaving? Where are you going?"

44

"Not sure. Colorado—maybe."

"Why, LeRoy? Why?" She couldn't hide the agitation in her voice.

"Ma, there's not much here for me. No future. Pay in Utah is low—you know that. Maybe twenty or thirty dollars a month with board—and the board's not much to brag about in most places. There's no excitement around here. I'm not a kid any more. Gotta be thinking about my future."

"Future?" She wanted to say how desperately she needed him, but she couldn't get the words out. Instead she said, "There's a future here."

"Who do you think you're joshing, Ma?" There was bitterness in his voice. "I look at the struggle you and Dad have had, and it don't look very good to me. Always somebody to cheat you out of what you've got coming— like the time you lost the homestead—"

"LeRoy, that's water under the bridge. We've pulled out of that."

"If it isn't some righteous saint getting the best of you, then it's the weather that's agin you, freezing the stock or the crops. I can't go it. I've got to get into something that brings me hard, solid gold in my hand. Thought maybe I could get a job in Telluride in the mines."

"LeRoy, you're barely eighteen—"

"Most fellas my age are on their own—a lot of 'em married."

She was silent for a long time, unable to put her tumbling thoughts into words that wouldn't sound preachy. She could see he was set in his thinking. Was he going to rendezvous with Mike Cassidy somewhere? "LeRoy, I don't want you going off alone. It's not good."

"I won't be alone. Eli Elder is going, too."

"Wait till your father comes home. He'll probably be back tomorrow night."

"Can't. I should've been gone today, but I wanted to say goodbye to you and the kids. I'll be putting my things together." He stood up and stretched. "Better turn in. Got a long ride ahead of me, and I'll need sleep."

He leaned over the rocker where she sat and planted a kiss on her forehead.

Who would know how Bob tossed and turned that night, torn with the thoughts of the path that lay before him? Mother lay still, staring into the darkness, wondering how she could delay him or reason further with this stubborn boy. That's all he was—a boy—in spite of his outward mature appearance. Well, you couldn't put an old head on young shoulders. The learning would be hard, but he'd have to learn his own lessons, even though she wanted desperately to shield him from the hard knocks.

Very early next morning, before anyone else was up, Bob gathered a few belongings together. Mother asked about a packhorse and camp outfit.

"Nope. Traveling light," he grinned. He ate a quick breakfast while Mother packed a few provisions, cheese, raisins. She was glad she had fresh bread to send with him and a jar of bullberry preserves. "Thanks, Ma, nothing like your bullberry p'serves. I'll miss it." She stifled the urge to tell him again how much they needed him and silently went to the bedroom. When she returned, she carried a blue woolen blanket.

"Not that, Ma. I know how much that blanket means to you."

"Your Grandfather Parker made it for you. You need it now, and you shall have it."

"It's too hot for a blanket now."

She insisted, "The nights are still cold. You'll need it."

He tiptoed over to the cradle and looked longingly at the baby. He didn't dare touch her, lest she awake. "I want to get away before anybody else is up, Ma. I can't stand to tell the kids goodbye."

She rolled the food first in a cloth, then tightly in the blue blanket, making a small, neat roll. He took it, picked up his hat, and without a word walked outside to his mare, Babe.

Mother followed him, checking the tears that threatened to spill over. He tied the bundle in his coat at the back of his saddle. Turning, he caught her up, lifting her feet from the ground as he always did when he bounced her to the table to crown her. He hugged her fiercely. "I'll be back soon, Ma, I promise."

"LeRoy, no matter what happens, hurry back. Always remember that your father and I need you as you need us."

Dash, the big yellow dog, ran panting to Bob, expecting to go along. Bob leaned down to pet him, digging affectionately at the scruff of his neck.

"No, old boy, you can't go. You're needed here." Tying a rope to his collar, he handed the rope to Mother. "Here, hold him so he can't follow." She recalled how the faithful old Dash had saved Blanche from drowning. Yes, she needed Dash; but oh, how much more she needed her son!

He swung up to the saddle, lifted his hat in a gallant salute, and turned his mare Babe toward the road, urging her to a smooth run; the young colt, Cornish, kept close like the little thoroughbred it was. Mother watched him go, past the poplar trees, thinking that in a way he might be better off to get away from the company he'd been keeping.

He turned to wave as he rode away from the yard, and saw his mother still holding the rope, Dash straining to follow. Hunching over his horse, he dared not look back again. She watched him fade into the landscape, and the puffs of dust settled. Little did she realize why he was leaving.

After tying Dash to the fence, she knelt down and idly pushed away dead leaves from the sweet williams. Digging lightly with her fingers in the moist earth gave her strength.

A baby's cry from the house broke the morning stillness. She was needed inside. As she approached the house, she could hear the voices of the other children. Her heart was heavy, but there was no time to weep. She must hide her grief and put on a smile for them. One son needed her no longer, but a houseful depended on her, and that was good. She couldn't smother the feeling that it would be a long time before she would see her firstborn again. How could she know it would be never?

The day dragged and the hours seemed endless in spite of the press of moving continuously from one task to another all day. When Dad came home that night, he was shocked to learn that Bob had gone.

"Dammit, I needed him. By gum, I wanted him to help clear that piece of ground on the south."

Next day Dad went into town and casually learned, through the grapevine, that an investigation had been started recently by men who knew their cattle, and some of them were missing. Several of their recognized cattle had turned up wearing brands of Charley and Fred, the pair who had been most friendly with Mike Cassidy the past couple of years. Mike had been gone for several months.

When confronted by the investigating committee, Charley and Fred produced a bill of sale from Robert LeRoy Parker.

Dad was furious and confronted his friend, the constable, James Wiley, who had drawn up the papers. There must be a way to clear Bob, Dad hoped desperately. Apparently Charley and Fred had talked Bob into giving them a bill of sale for the cattle so that it would appear Bob had been their owner and that he had sold them to Charley and Fred, who would then be in the clear. The finger of suspicion would be pointed squarely at Bob. And Charley and Fred could stay with their families instead of fleeing. Bob had wanted to leave the country anyhow. So he could clear out now, let the talk settle, and come back later when everyone had forgotten the whole affair.

Dad stormed at Wiley. "How could you do this, Jim? You know LeRoy didn't have money to buy a cow, let alone a herd. And now this makes him the guilty party. I wouldn't have treated a son of yours like that. This is a fine thing after all our years of friendship."

48

Constable Wiley replied, "Max, don't take it so hard. Charley and Fred have their families they couldn't leave. Bob could take the blame, go away for a few years, and come back and nothing will be done. The rightful owners have their cattle back now."

"LeRoy can never come back here and hold his head up," Dad fumed.

"Let it lay, Max. It's over. If you try to stir up trouble, a bishop's trial will be called. It'll only make matters worse. You lost one bishop's trial, if you recall."

"How could I forget?" Dad grumbled.

"I wouldn't risk another if I was you. If you bring your boy back for a trial, it'll be his word against that of two other men. You haven't got a chance, Max."

Dad could see the sense of this. It was useless to waste time trying to locate the boy. He had no idea how he could find him. The ranch demanded attention. A big family was depending on him. He'd have to let things lie for the present. Dad recalled that Bob had wanted to go with Mike Cassidy several months ago when he had pulled out. Mike had said to Bob, "No, the place for you is here on the farm. You're too good a kid to go where I'm going." The outlaw had been far more of a man than these righteous "friends," Dad reflected. Mike, the outlaw, wouldn't have pushed the boy into a shady deal.

Bob was gone. Mother's friends respected her silence and never once brought up the matter. Not many people knew the facts, and my parents couldn't see where it would do any good to tell what they knew. Charley and Fred didn't have a good reputation anyhow, and it would only harm their families to say more. Once Charley's wife twitted my oldest sister about Bob's going to the bad. That was too much. Even though the family had been sworn to silence, Sister turned to the woman and angrily told her if it hadn't been for Charley and Fred, Bob wouldn't be in trouble. And that ended that.

Bob had a rigid code, one he never violated even in the tightest spots. He was loyal to his friends, his family and his employers. I have often been informed by his associates that he was courteous and respectful to all women and that any girl was safe with him. He was kind to animals and was a fine horseman. He was a man's man. He commanded respect from them all, even those who were on the opposite side of the law. All his life children adored him. He had a natural way with them. Wherever Bob went, the farmers and ranchers welcomed him. He was pleasant and witty, good company, trustworthy, compassionate.

These are reports from law-abiding citizens who were his friends. They are not my observations. Had he been less of a man on that June morning in 1884, he would not have taken the blame so that two men could remake their own lives.

Some time after Bob left home, Mr. Kittleman's horses were stolen. Writers have jumped to the conclusion that Bob got away with them, but nothing could be further from the truth. One of Bob's most outstanding virtues was his loyalty to friends and family. Bob would as soon have stolen from his own father as from Jim Kittleman. As a matter of fact, after Bob left home that morning, he stopped and talked to Mr. Kittleman, who tried to coax him out of going. Then Bob headed north and east about six miles to Kingston, where he met Eli Elder, and they were on their way.[3]

Writers have also recorded that Bob was jailed for stealing a saddle. This is not true. He owned his own horse, and Mike had given him a saddle; so he had no reason to steal one.

3. Many writers have stated that Bob escaped from the jail in Panguitch, Utah, just before he went to Colorado. However, the County Clerk reports that there is no record of his arrest and imprisonment there.

Although I was a baby at the time all this happened, through the years Mother repeated the details many, many times in almost the same words, until it became as clear as if I, too, had experienced it. She never got over the heartache. Nor would our family ever be the same again. Our eldest brother was gone.

At thirteen, he had assumed the work and the responsibilities of a man; as he grew older, he watched both our father and mother leave home for periods of time to scratch out enough money to keep our family subsisting; he had smarted under the realization that a "righteous Saint" had taken away from us our hard-homesteaded piece of land; he had admired an outlaw's skill with cattle, horses, and guns; he had sympathized with the small homesteader who "mavericked" cattle from land-usurping cattle barons—had even accepted the blame for the actions of two of them; and he had craved a freedom he could never experience at our little ranch in Circle Valley.

Were his deep love for Mother, his affection for us kids, and his memory of good times with the family enough to override all these influences and keep him from straying too far and too long?

Life in Telluride
Chapter 5

For several years Telluride, Colorado, had been the land of promise for pioneer boys of Utah. It was said that the name Telluride was derived from the phrase "to hell you ride."

When Bob rode into Telluride that summer, it was a wide-open, roaring mining town. Never before had he seen so many people milling around. Swaggering cowboys walked the board sidewalks with their own peculiar rolling gait, acquired from being on a horse for endless hours. Eager miners hurried in and out of the bank and saloons. Loud laughter and boisterous talk resounded from the swinging doors of the saloons. Trading stores bulged with supplies waiting to be purchased by the town's teeming and changing population.

Bob's eyes popped at the sight of the large sums of money that frequently changed hands. He tingled with excitement as he watched the gamblers and dance-hall girls. Here was living—here was excitement beyond his imagination.[1]

He found a suitable pasture for his horse and colt, Babe and Cornish. Almost immediately he found employment packing ore from the mine, down the moun-

---

1. All the events of this chapter about Bob's life in Telluride were told to me by my father.

tain to the mill on mules. Bob stood about five feet nine inches tall and was well built, but on the slender side. (Writers have usually described him as being rather heavy, but that was not true in his younger years.) Although the work was demanding, he enjoyed it, quickly learning how to put the packs on the mules with skill, and he surely knew how to handle the mules. He was well paid for a job well done. In the evenings he joined his friends in the saloons.

Pretty girls in the dance halls were very different from the ones at home. And the jingle of goldpieces in his pockets gave him a sense of security; but he didn't hang onto them very long. Occasionally he sent money home to help out. He knew things were still tight there, but letters from home were stabilizers for him.

He had no need for two horses, so he sold Babe and kept the colt Cornish at a ranch down on the river. At first, he checked on Cornish frequently. However, as other interests absorbed him, he paid the colt less and less attention until its second year. One day he went up to the fence and called, "Come on, Cornish." Obediently the colt trotted over to him. He went often then, to make friends with the sleek young horse.

The following spring, when Cornish was three years old, the time had come to break him. Bob caught the colt and broke it to lead a couple of times. This colt was beginning to shape up beautifully. The rancher had taken a real liking to Cornish and wanted to buy him, but Bob wouldn't sell. One evening after work, Bob took the colt out of the pasture to start breaking it.

The envious rancher swore out a warrant for Bob's arrest, accusing him of horse stealing, knowing that a number of men could testify in court that as long as they had known the brown colt, it had been at his ranch. Bob could not point to a brand, so the rancher thought this was a good chance to pick up a fine horse.

Bob was jailed in Montrose, a town not far from Telluride. But his friends knew he was innocent. They wired Dad that Bob needed help.

Dad left immediately. When he arrived at Montrose, he found Bob sitting in his cell, reading a magazine, with the door wide open. When Bob heard approaching footsteps he looked up, and his mouth dropped open. "Dad!" he shouted, "what in hell are you doing here?"

"By gum, young man," Dad replied, "I might ask you the same question. What's this all about?" He scratched his head. "This is the first time I ever heard of a prisoner being imprisoned behind an open cell door."

Bob grinned. "They're not afraid I'll escape. They know I haven't taken anything that wasn't mine. I plan to stay right here until I get my horse."

Dad's presence changed the whole complexion of the situation, for Bob was backed by his father, clearly a man of integrity and authority. When character witnesses came forward and volunteered their testimony, the rancher was defeated.

After the trial, Dad urged, "Come home with me. Your mother's never been the same. We need you. You wouldn't believe how cute little Lula is, trying to keep up with the others. Baby Mark is growing fast and you haven't even seen him. We all miss you. By gum, Son, the kids need you too. This is no kind of a life for you."

Bob was silent, an inner struggle going on. He longed for the security of his family. Then he recalled his trapped feeling in Utah: closed in, nothing he could get his hands on, no money, no excitement. He couldn't go back to that. "Tell you what, Dad, give me a little longer to save more money, and I'll be home." He pressed some gold-pieces in his father's hand. "For Ma." He swallowed the lump in his throat, not daring to say more.

"Your mother will appreciate the money, but it's no substitute for you."

Dad went back to Circleville alone. Money in Circleville was still very scarce; so a few years later Dad took my brother Arthur and went to Telluride, intending to open a livery stable. My oldest sister went to keep house for them. However, the altitude was too high for Dad, and he returned home. They gave up the idea of the livery stable, but Arthur stayed in Telluride to work, as did my sister.

Arthur was a fine horseman and a good jockey. At the Fourth of July celebration, the horse he was riding in the big race fell and broke Arthur's leg. He was taken to the hotel, and the doctor was called. Arthur never regained consciousness and died a few days later. We always thought he died from a blood clot.[2] Several Circleville men were working in Telluride at the time; the Wiley brothers (Heber and Jim) and Lew Davis were there. They took care of everything.

I remember when we got the news of Arthur's death. Uncle Dan Gillies (Mother's brother who ran the post office at Circleville) brought the message, which had been sent on from the Salina telegraph station. Mother was distraught. It was impossible to reach Telluride in time for Arthur's funeral. He was buried before we received the word. Even though I was a little girl, I can still see Mother pacing in the fields, trying to wear out her grief. But around us she put on a good front and hid her sorrow.

After Bob was acquitted for stealing his own horse Cornish, he left Telluride and drifted up into Wyoming, working at odd jobs but trying to find more exciting employment than he'd had at Telluride. During this time, he made friends with a number of men who later became part of the Wild Bunch. So he was not in Telluride when Dad and Arthur went over, nor at the time of Arthur's death.

On January 6, 1889, the eleventh baby arrived at our house. Sometime later a letter came from Bob in which he enclosed one hundred dollars and suggested that we name the baby Nina Grace. I do not know of his sending money home after that. I think this is significant. Until then he had earned honest money, and he respected

2. We have been unable to obtain a death certificate, but I have been to Arthur's grave in Telluride.

our parents so much that he never sent the later "tainted money." It must have given him a feeling of satisfaction to be able to earn enough money to help his family—enough satisfaction that he had no desire to return to a life of scratching out an existence.

Genesis of
an Outlaw
Chapter 6

     Bob returned to Telluride, where he got a job. It was probably early spring of that year when Matt Warner came into town with a fast racehorse named Betty. When Bob and Matt met, they were surprised to learn they were both from Utah. Matt Warner came from Levan, Utah, his real name being Willard Erastus Christiansen.[1]

     Bob quit his job to join Matt in the excitement of horseracing, the main spectator sport in those days. An excellent rider, Bob was the winning jockey many times.

     At Cortez they ran into Tom McCarty, an old friend of Matt's. After several successful races, they made the mistake of matching Betty against a one-eyed Indian pony, White Face. Again Betty won the race, but the cowboys were in for trouble. The Indians couldn't quite understand the defeat and refused to leave. The cowboys, as winners of the race, were entitled to take possession of White Face and a load of Indian blankets. Tom McCarty started to throw the blankets onto the buckboard. A big warrior grabbed them and forcibly took them away.

---

1. Matt Warner and Murray E. King, *The Last of The Bandit Riders* Caldwell, Idaho: The Caxton Printers, Ltd., 1940), p. 22. On page 107 he also states that Bob was going under the name of Roy Parker, and he gives his name as George LeRoy Parker. Of course, the George is wrong. Of significance is the fact that he had dropped Robert or Bob, his real name.

Tom was hot-headed. A quirt was fastened to his wrist. Without a moment's thought, he gave the Indian a severe lashing in front of his companion warriors. No one could do a thing like that and get away with it. Because of their number, those Indians could wipe out the cowboys in less time than it took to tell about it. The cowboys instantly pulled out their Winchesters and cocked them. The Indians knew if they retaliated at that moment, their losses would be too great. So they allowed the cowboys to back slowly away, holding their cocked Winchesters.

With distance between them, the cowboys raced for Tom's cabin, riding all night, and reached it before daylight. They knew that Indians are superstitious about night fighting; but by daylight, true to their expectations, they spotted about fifteen Indians riding toward the cabin. The warriors were willing to forget what had happened the day before if they could have White Face.

"Injun bet White Face," Bob reasoned. "White man win White Face. White Face belong white man."

"Injun take White Face back," the Chief said firmly.

Tom yelled into their faces, "Get out! Race-horse belong white man."

As quick as triggered lightning, the Indian turned his Winchester on Tom, but quicker than that Tom drew his six-shooter and shot. The Indian slid off his horse to the ground. The cowboys covered the group of Indians with their guns as the Indians loaded the dead man on his pony and rode away silently.[2] This went against Bob's grain. Killing wasn't part of the game for him, and he was sick inside. But he stayed with the men.

"Easy come, easy go." Their winnings from races slipped through their fingers in high living. But they eased their consciences by giving a share to poverty-stricken nesters. However, no one else would match Betty

2. Warner and King, pp. 111-15. The background information for the bulk of the foregoing comes from Matt Warner.

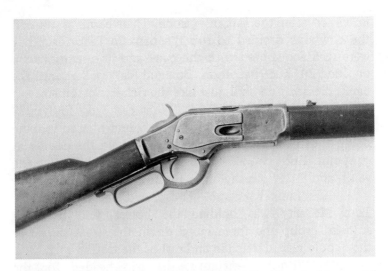

Butch Cassidy's Winchester 73 44-40 Saddle Ring Carbine, serial # 64876. *Courtesy of Jim Earle, who owns the gun.*

in a race after the Indian episode. Their earnings cut off, the cowboys decided to rob the bank in Telluride. They were well acquainted with the bank and its operations. So on June 24, 1889, at noon, Bob and Matt walked into the bank, dressed fit to kill, just like the richest customers.

The cashier smiled. "What can I do for you?" Suddenly his face grew ashen as he found himself looking down the barrel of a gun. While Matt held the cashier at gunpoint, Bob scooped the money into a sack, visited the vault, and the two rushed into the street.

"Bank robbers!" The crowd heard the shout. Tom McCarty was holding the horses, and before a stunned group the three raced down the street as fast as they could ride, darting in and out of the traffic.

Without resistance, the trio headed for the Mancos Mountains where Matt had his herd of horses. However, as they headed up over a trail, at a crossroads they met two fellows they knew from Telluride. Without stopping to pass the time of day, they spurred their horses and were on a dead run for their destination. Too late, they realized this would be their downfall. If they had been nonchalant and had stopped to visit, they would not have been suspect. But their actions of ignoring the horsemen and riding on at a wild pace alerted the men that something was wrong. When the acquaintances arrived in town, they put two and two together and could then furnish the names and descriptions of the bank robbers.

This put Tom, Matt, and Bob on the wanted list. They had crossed the line into outlawry. The only way they could make a living now was to rob in earnest. They had taken $31,000, which meant roughly $10,000 each. But what could they do with it? They couldn't afford to be seen for fear of being arrested.

As mentioned before, Bob never sent money home after he hit the outlaw trail; and wandering as he did, in hiding much of the time, he was beyond the stabilizing influence of home by mail service.

After the Telluride Bank robbery, the group split up. Bob was determined to go straight.

Mounted on his horse, Bob had nowhere to go.

Telluride Bank, August, 1899. *Courtesy of the Library, State Historical Society, Colorado.*

He was all alone in the world. No one knew or cared, he assumed, where he was or what he was doing. Perhaps if he had written home oftener—but what could you say in letters when you were doing things you couldn't "'fess up to"? How he longed to head straight west for Circleville, put his mistakes behind him, and start all over again. But now, more than ever, after the Telluride robbery, that was impossible. Any hope of a decent future was buried in his past mistakes. He couldn't disgrace his family.[3]

His horse ambled on with little direction from its rider, up one mountain and down the other side, through weeks in desolate canyons, then up into high mountains where he felt he was on top of the whole world. The silence was almost more than he could bear at times— no one to share his dark thoughts. If only he could talk to Ma. Perhaps he could slip into the ranch, get the help he needed, and be on his way without being noticed by others. He continued west, but the closer he got to home, the weaker he felt.

Maybe they were still looking for him after that Charley and Fred deal. Avoiding any roads that might lead to Beaver or Circleville, he found himself quite a distance west in the railroad town of Milford.

Much to his surprise, he ran into his brother Dan who was working there. They were overjoyed to see each other and went into a tavern for a long lunch.

Following that meeting, Bob was more convinced than ever that he must steer clear of home for the time being. As his horse meandered along the road, he had plenty of thinking time. He'd have to change his name completely. Mike Cassidy had taught him well—too well. So it would be natural to take the name of Cassidy. He'd al-

3. Bob later told us of these feelings.

ready dropped the Robert and had been known as Roy Parker to the friends he'd made in Telluride and later.

He came to a fork in the road and the horse stopped. If he followed one road, it would eventually lead him to Circleville. Instead of turning his horse's head toward home, as he longed to do, he headed north and east toward Brown's Hole.

Brown's Hole (also known as Brown's Park) is an area nestled in the vast rock country bordering eastern Utah, the northwestern corner of Colorado, and a bit of southern Wyoming, thus offering legal immunity to outlaws, by their dodging from one bordering state to another. There was little law in the Park; but there was usually work to be done, and a good cowhand or farmhand could find employment for as long as he wished.

So Bob had made the decision that would keep him for many years from returning to the straight life. Ironically, the love he felt for his family, creating in him a yearning to go to them, also kept him from them—and directed him further into lawless activities.

I have wondered why, when my brother's reputation as a jockey suffered, he did not turn to wrangling permanently to earn a living instead of only now and then, between robberies, finding work as a ranch hand.

At Brown's Park and Rock Springs
Chapter 7

That summer of 1889 at Brown's Hole, Bob met Charley Crouse and introduced himself as a friend of Matt Warner. Mr. Crouse was a freighter and also had a big spread in Brown's Hole. In about 1909 he acquired a saloon but was not a saloonkeeper when Bob first arrived, as has often been written.[1]

"I need work—I can do any kind of range work," Bob volunteered, then added, "I'm pretty good at horseracing, too." Bob had previously heard of Charley's reputation and his appetite for racing.

"I'll see what we can do," Charley said. But nothing turned up right away, and Bob soon found himself working as a ranch hand at the Bassett Ranch. Herbert and Mary Eliza Chamberlain Bassett had five children: Josie, Sam, Ann, Eb and George.[2] They had come West from Arkansas in search of better health for Herbert, who suffered from asthma. Herbert was educated and religious.

1. Personal interview on May 6, 1972, in Jensen, Utah, with Crawford MacKnight, a son of Josie Bassett MacKnight Morris, who knew Charley Crouse.

2. A personal record book in Herbert Bassett's own handwriting, now in possession of Crawford MacKnight, Jensen, Utah, lists names, birthdates, and places. Mary Eliza's name has been given in such a variety of ways by various writers that it needs verification. Here is the primary source.

This family reminded Bob so much of his own in Circleville that he felt he had found a home away from home. He liked to read, and the many good books in the Bassett library were an open invitation. The hired hands lived in the nearby bunkhouse which slept four. On Sundays and some evenings the residents gathered at the Bassett's for worship and social gatherings. Their organ also reminded Bob of home and the way his parents sang with their family. This was the social hub of the valley, and Mrs. Bassett enjoyed her role. Josie, in her teens, and Ann Bassett, four years younger, were substitutes for Bob's own sisters. Josie was usually busy indoors, but Ann hated housework and tagged after Bob, which flattered him immensely.

Herbert Bassett's grandson, Crawford MacKnight, says that horse races and dances were the principal means of recreation. He gives an account of a race Bob took part in:

> One day there was a mile race between Charley Crouse's and Roy Parker's (Butch Cassidy's) horses. Butch ran one for old Buckskin Ed Whitworth. He'd trained the horse himself. They was kinda afraid it was a put-up job. Crouse's racehorse had been trained to look away and then whirl and start. This would put the other person off guard. Well, old Whitworth and Butch got onto it, and they trained Butch's horse to do the same things—face away from the racetrack then whirl and take off. Butch won the race by several lengths. If I remember right, there was about $3,000 on the race and the winner would take both horses. So Buckskin Ed got two horses out of the deal: his own horse back and Crouse's horse. There was a lot of people there—people from miles around. Horse racing was about the only entertainment they had.[3]

Ann Bassett said of Bob: "A dancing party was given at the Charles Allen ranch to celebrate the winning

3. MacKnight interview.

68

of a race. The youthful jockey stabled the horse, joined us at supper, then went quietly to bed, without sharing in the jubilant merry-making that went on until dawn streaked the sky." [4]

Minnie Crouse Rasmussen (Charley Crouse's daughter) told of Bob's courtesy: "I was a teenager when Cassidy rode into the yard one day, and saw that we were trying to get a newborn colt on its feet. He helped us get the colt walking and stayed around for several minutes to make certain it was up to stay, before he walked into the house to talk with father." [5]

After an extended stay at the Bassett's Ranch, Bob left in search of better employment. He mounted his horse early, before the girls were up. Goodbyes were difficult for him, and this was almost like leaving home all over again.

Regretfully he recalled that morning in June, 1884, when he had galloped off into the unknown. It had changed his life. He couldn't help wondering where he'd be and what he'd be doing if he'd stayed at home. Rock Springs was seventy-five miles away. He could get work there in the mines and return to Brown's Park when he wanted to.

But when he arrived in Rock Springs, he learned the work there was only in coal mines, and that wasn't for him. Looking around town for work, he bumped into a man by the name of William Gottsche who ran a butcher shop. He needed someone reliable. This was better than coal mining; so Bob took the job. My brother had a disarming way with people. It wasn't long before he had befriended nearly everyone in town. He always gave good measure with the meat, and housewives had the highest confidence in him; children adored him.

4. Letter to the Duward Campbells of Brown's Park from Ann Bassett. Butch Cassidy was that jockey. Published in *Deseret News,* Salt Lake City, Utah, July 25, 1970.

5. Article, *Deseret News,* July 25, 1970.

Since the Telluride bank robbery, Bob was uneasy about his name. He answered to George Parker or Ed Cassidy. Then in a casual way people began calling him Butch. This rolled off the tongue smoothly with Cassidy. And Butch Cassidy came into being.

(Matt Warner tells a different story of how Butch acquired his name. But when Bob first went into Brown's Park, he used the name Roy Parker. And since the incident Matt Warner relates happened before Bob went to Brown's Park, I'm inclined to believe the name "Butch" came from his work in Rock Springs.)

Wherever Bob went, he worked, never expecting something for nothing. But things were going too smoothly to last.

Even though Bob was not large, he was strong and quick. One night in a saloon brawl he saved the life of Douglas A. Preston, a foremost criminal lawyer.[6] From that time Preston became permanently indebted to Butch and defended not only him but later on members of his gang.

In Rock Springs Harry Stephen Parker[7] (known as Harry S.) was marshall. If my brother's name, or change of names, had caused identification problems before, the similarity of Bob's name and the marshall's family name

6. Personal interview with Pete Parker, Feb. 20, 1973, of Jackson, Wyoming.

7. About 1870 George Parker (Sr.) brought his large family from England to the United States. Of ten children, his sons, Harry Stephen and George, were the only ones to go West. They were not Mormons.

Harry S. became deputy and U.S. Marshall of Wyoming. Then he became town marshall in the wild railroad town of Rock Springs, Wyoming. In later life he became a railroad detective in Salt Lake City, then moved to Bountiful, Utah, where he farmed for a time. This was too quiet a life for him, so the family returned to Rock Springs, where he was employed as outside foreman for the Union Pacific #1 Mine. He was chief prospector for Union Pacific until a short time before his death. His son, Harry George Parker, served as City Treasurer for one term, was elected mayor for one

Rock Springs, Wyoming, in 1896. *Courtesy of Sweetwater County Museum, Green River, Wyoming.*

hopelessly tangled identities in Rock Springs, as we shall later see.

While Bob was working in Gottsche's butcher shop, the town of Rock Springs was alive with foreigners who had filtered into the area because of the railroad and the mines. On payday brawny emigrants from Finland who worked in the mines filled the saloons. The gambling hall was on Union Pacific Railroad property.

On a particular day Butch was cutting meat for John Maulson, who ran a ranch twenty miles south of Rock Springs and had a small butcher shop in Rock Springs. The drunken, formidable Finns were acting like crazy men. The Union Pacific people sent for their "law man," George Pickering, but he was not to be found. So they called for Marshall Harry S. Parker to come and stop the fighting and destruction.

Bob happened to see Marshall Parker enter the gambling hall. From the din inside he knew the lawman would be killed. At that moment Pickering arrived, carrying his rifle. Clutching his meat cleaver, Bob hurried into the hall to see the drunken Finns descending on the poor marshall with broken bottles, knives—anything they could get their hands on. Bob shouted above the noise. Seeing Bob holding his ominous meat cleaver high and Pickering fully armed, the Finns shrank back. Order was restored, and the marshall's life had been saved.

One night Bob was enjoying himself in a saloon, with not many people present, chatting with a fellow who was known to be a confirmed drunkard. Since it was payday, the fellow had a large amount of money on him. After a few drinks he was thoroughly inebriated, and his money spilled carelessly over the bar. A number of people observed Bob talking to him and noticed the loose money. Bob walked away. The bartender put a piece of gum in his mouth and chewed it hastily. The drunkard sank onto the bar in a stupor, scattering the coins. The bartender slipped

term (1922-23) and served several terms as City Councilman in the 1920s.

Harry George had a son, Pete Parker, who has shared the details of my brother's life in Rock Springs, as given.

Rock Springs, Wyoming, before 1915. *Courtesy of Sweetwater County Museum, Green River, Wyoming.*

a wad of gum on each shoe sole and, with his arm, unobtrusively shoved the tiny goldpieces from the counter to the floor. As he walked, the gum collected the money on his shoes.[8]

Bob was arrested for rolling the drunkard. It was a case clearly based on circumstantial evidence.[9] Bob was so furious at being falsely arrested for such a petty, sneaking crime that he swore vengeance.

The more Bob saw, the more disgusted he became with the laws that were supposed to protect people and their rights. He came to feel they protected only the man who already had more money than he knew what to do with and more herds than he could keep track of. He couldn't forget how his own parents' land had been jumped. The underdog always got the raw end of a deal. The little homesteader, more often than not, was driven off by the big man who had enough cash to see that the land office was on his side and that he ended up with huge tracts of choice rangeland.

From his own observations, Bob felt that banks and railroad companies were also out to take away the land from the poor man to use for their own greedy purposes. His bitterness against money factions deepened.

In Rock Springs, Marshall Harry S. Parker had a son, Harry George Parker. Also in town was the marshall's brother, George Parker. At that time, my brother Bob was going by the name of George Parker a good bit of the time. Although the following explanation is confusing, it may give a clue as to why he picked that particular name. George Parker (brother of the marshall) was frequently stirring up some devilment, and my brother was trying his own wings. There were undoubtedly cases of mistaken identity because both were known by the same name. This sometimes kept Bob from suspicion.

8. Pete Parker.

9. Arrest records have been searched to no avail. Some of them have been lost.

Bob had a number of renegade friends in the surrounding territory, and they banded together to take revenge for the false arrest of rolling the drunkard. They cleared out of town but remained in the general vicinity, stirring up a good bit of excitement. This was the group called the Wild Bunch. Young Harry George Parker, the son of Marshall Parker, also knew Douglas A. Preston, the lawyer friend of Butch Cassidy, alias George Parker. A considerable amount of communication passed back and forth between Preston and Butch. Preston lured the Marshall's son, Harry, to be their go-between. Preston's offices were in the Labor Temple in Rock Springs. In the middle of the block behind the office of Preston was a livery stable. One day Preston asked young Harry Parker if he would get a livery horse and ride up Horse Thief Canyon (later called Superior). That was a pretty scary trail, and Harry coaxed his friend, Jim Sloan, to go along with him. Preston gave young Harry a goldpiece and guaranteed the livery charges. Harry split the money with Jim on that first ride.

They arrived at dusk at the place where Preston had directed them. Rock precipices loomed before them, and they hunched over their horses in fear, afraid they'd missed their rendezvous. Harry peered anxiously into the near darkness but couldn't see anyone. All of a sudden, a man stepped from behind a big cedar tree.

"Looking for someone?" the bearded man asked.

The hair stood up on Harry's and Jim's necks. Harry's voice quavered. "Yes, a man I'm supposed to meet right here."

"You know who?"

"No. Douglas Preston sent me."

"I'm your man."

The bearded man lit a match and read the message. Then he scrawled a message on a piece of paper, sealed it, and gave it to Harry with instructions to return it to Preston. The bearded man gave Harry another twenty-dollar goldpiece with the words, "Don't mention this to anyone at all. Personal business."

Harry made several rides for Preston. One was to Linwood, Utah, which took several days. He recognized the same man at his destination, although that time he didn't have his beard. Harry received a double eagle ($20) at the end of each ride.

At first young Harry kept his money under cover; then he started treating his friends, and the marshall began to wonder how his son had become so rich. Harry tried to avoid the questions, but at last his father pinned him down; the story was out. That was the end of the road and of the goldpieces for Harry. But he and Preston remained lifelong friends. And of course, by now Harry knew who the man on the other end was.[10]

The Wild Bunch would swoop into town to celebrate for reasons which were never hard to find, and no one dared stand in their way. The Commercial Hotel in Rock Springs was the target for some of these celebrations. When the Bunch was high on liquor, there was no telling what might happen. The Kierles, who ran the hotel, were very careful on these occasions and let in only a few special friends and customers. Any communication to the outside was on foot. On this particular night someone ran across town to get Marshall Parker. The Bunch had their horses tied at the hitching post across the street from the rear of the hotel, where the post office now is. Knowing someone had gone for the law, they mounted their horses and were on their way out of town when the Marshall arrived. He shouted at Butch, "Butch, stop right where you are or I'll shoot."

Butch called back, "Hurry up; we're trying to get out of town. We won't cause any more trouble."

10. Interview with Pete Parker on February 20, 1973.

Douglas A. Preston, Attorney. *Courtesy of Sweetwater County Museum, Green River, Wyoming.*

Pete Parker holding Butch's watch.

Marshall Parker was a big, broad man. As he rode up on his horse, Butch was timing him by his pocket watch which he held in his hand. Marshall Parker said, "You've caused enough trouble. I'll let you leave, but you've got to pay some kind of a fine for what you do to this town."

He reached out and grabbed Butch's watch. Butch turned his horse and joined the Bunch as they galloped on. The Marshall gave the watch to the town for damages and then bought it back. His son, Harry Parker, inherited the valuable watch; then it went to his son, Pete Parker.

I don't know how or where, but Bob met Elzy (pronounced Elzuh) Lay, a tall, good-looking young fellow. He and Bob found much in common. Both had been brought up in good homes by parents who loved them and had exposed them to religious training. Elzy has been labeled by writers as "the Boston-educated outlaw." The truth of the matter is that he probably never saw Boston. He was born William Elzy Lay in MacArthur, Vinton County, Ohio, November 25, 1868, the son of James L. Lay and Mary Jane Bellew.[11]

The family moved to Laird, Colorado, and then to Woodruff, Kansas. In his early childhood, Elzy ran around in Ohio with a boy named William McGinnis, and this became one of Elzy's aliases in later years. He left home for the West and settled for ranch work in Brown's Park. This was probably where Elzy and Butch met.

11. Information concerning Elzy Lay was received from family records in the possession of Marvel Lay Murdock, daughter of Elzy Lay, living in Heber City, Utah, and her son, Harvey Murdock, Salt Lake City, Utah. For more information, see Appendix B.

Elzy met Matt Warner, also a friend of Butch's, and worked for him mavericking and breaking horses. From Charley Crouse Elzy learned his skill as a horseman. He also did general ranch work for the Bassetts.

Butch and Elzy were looking for excitement, but neither was a killer by nature. Theirs became a lifelong friendship.

Through the next few years, Bob was in and out of Brown's Park. It was a good place to slip into when the trail was hot elsewhere. Vernal was fifty miles away from Brown's Park; Rock Springs, Wyoming, was seventy-five miles, and Hahn's Peak, Colorado, was nearly a hundred. The dangerous mountain passes and the Green River were good natural barriers. The people in Brown's Park entertained a special disdain for the powerful cattle barons who wanted to take over the land for their big herds. Lawmen were not treated hospitably, and any of the local people would willingly harbor Bob and other outlaws. Bob occupied a special spot in their hearts. Wherever he worked, he did an honest day's labor for his pay. They trusted him.

Josie Bassett Morris stated in a tape on file at Dinosaur National Monument, Jensen, Utah:

. . . I knew Butch Cassidy a long, long time and so did my father before we ever believed that he was on that life. My father would never believe for a long time. He said, "That fella is not that kind of a man." He was a quiet young man nobody knew. Well, he broke horses for different people, worked with cattle and everything. Never got drunk . . .

I have received from many sources similar testimonials to the trustworthiness and seeming stability of my brother—testimonials that have led me to ask again and again how such a man could have become a wanted criminal.

Butch's old cabin in Brown's Park. *Courtesy of Stella Dickey, Lander, Wyoming.*

In Prison
Chapter 8

      Bob went to work for the EA Outfit in the Wind River, Wyoming, country. Eugene Amaretti, an Italian, owned the EA Outfit and had 40,000 head of cattle ranging from the Shoshone Indian Reservation (about five miles from Lander) to the headwaters of Wind River, a distance of one hundred and fifty miles. Hired at the same time was a young fellow by the name of Al Hainer. [1]

      Bob and Al decided to homestead together.

      The winter of 1892-93 was a severe one. The weather wasn't the only trouble; a flu epidemic was raging throughout the West. But whether a man could get on his feet or not, chores had to be done. Reports have come to me from more than one source of how Bob moved from ranch to ranch taking over the heavy work where a rancher was stricken. He stayed until the man was on his feet and able to take over.

      Among Bob's special friends were John C. Simpson and his wife Margaret, who ranched in the vicinity of Lander. Mrs. Simpson possessed a knowledge of simple medicine and herbs. She concocted remedies, and Bob delivered them far and near to the sufferers. Along with the medicine, he carried such good cheer that Mrs.

---

1. Letter from Ida Simpson Redmond, daughter of John and Margaret Simpson. Hainer's name is listed in court records as Al or Albert Hainer, Haynor, or Hayner.

Simpson reported he saved more than one man's life with his hopeful encouragement. She stated that when Bob was around, the water buckets were always full and the wood-box running over.[2]

In Wyoming, Butch seemingly lived a normal life. He enjoyed squiring the girls, and the girls thought him a good catch. All her life, Ada Calvert considered him tops. Her father ran a store, and Butch and his friends traded there. Ada said he was always "full of devilment," and was usually dreaming up tricks to play on his buddies.

"He was no angel," she said, "but he never drank. And when his gang got too much, he'd put them down." She recalled that he stole horses when he was in trouble. He stole some from her father, Kirk Calvert, when he and his sons and hired hands were on roundup. The Wild Bunch swooped down on them near Baggs, Wyoming, and took off with all their horses, thirty of them, stealing them at night from a corral. "My brother wanted to get a posse and kill him, but my father just said to 'leave Butch alone.' Later Butch paid my father for the horses."

Ada relates that Butch and the Wild Bunch "found it convenient to hang around Baggs and Craig, Colorado." If they were hunted for law-breaking in Wyoming, they could slip over the border into Colorado, and vice versa. When things were quiet, they'd camp outside of town, then at night they'd slip into town, get some women, and dance.

At one time, Ada recalls, the river overflowed and the Calvert store was flooded. Butch and his boys swam the rising river to help them out. Ada loved to ride

2. Letter from Ida Simpson Redmond, daughter of John and Margaret Simpson to me.

Ada Calvert Piper, about 1960. Ada knew Butch in the Wind River country. *Courtesy of Robert V. Thompson Photography, Clinton, Iowa.*

Dora Lamoureaux Robertson in 1967. Dora and Butch saw each other frequently when he was in Lander, Wyoming. *Courtesy of Dora's daughter, Mrs. Irene Lane, Lander, Wyoming.*

horses and help her father round up the cattle and sometimes Butch helped her.[3]

Dora Lamoreaux was a girlfriend of his. In her later years she was asked by a nosey inquirer what they did on dates.

"We rode horseback and we danced," she replied. His questions became a little more pointed and finally he came right out and asked her if they "necked." (He was too young to know it was spooning in those days.) She was insulted and crisply replied, "Young man, I'll have you know he was a gentleman and I was a lady."[4] That ended the inquisition.

Maude Baker Eldredge, who lives in Craig, Colorado, is the daughter of C. E. Baker, one of the early settlers in the northwestern part of Colorado, and one of its leading citizens. In the history she has compiled, and which was published serially beginning February 12, 1971, in *The Daily Press*, she records the following:

> When C. E. Baker first came to the Fortification Valley as a homesteader tenderfoot from upper State New York, Butch Cassidy, temporarily employed at the Charlie Ayer's ranch, just south of Dixon, Wyoming, was the first top stock and ranch hand to offer his know-how and neighborly assistance to the Baker's Homesteading Venture.
>
> Cassidy, a native of the ranch country near Circleville, Utah, was considered a prize hand, by the various ranchers by whom he was employed at various seasons of the year.
>
> In the years that followed and prior to the zenith when Cassidy had earned for himself the reputation of 'King of the Wild Bunch,' C. E. Baker and Cassidy, being the same age, in their mid-twenties, shared an unusual and warm friendship.

3. Article about Ada Calvert Piper in the *Rawlins Daily Times*, December 9, 1967.

4. Letter to me from Dora's friend, Bill Marion, Lander, Wyoming.

Margaret Sullivan Simpson and John Porter Simpson, friends of Butch, on their fiftieth wedding anniversary in 1915. They were married on December 25, 1865. *Courtesy of Dorothy Hubbard.*

In the formative years of the ranch C. E. Baker leaned heavily on Cassidy's expert knowledge of Western homesteading. Years later, when Hi Bernard, foreman for the Two-Bar outfit, was complimenting Baker on the continued progress of the ranch, Baker was quick to place the credit squarely where it belonged. He said, "This ranch owes much to Butch Cassidy. Without his expert guidance and his encouragement, doubtless there would have been many blunders. You see, Bernard, farming in New York State is at pole's length from ranching in the West. I came here as a tenderfoot."

This again exemplifies the C. E. Baker philosophy:

At a time when feelings were riding high, with a war raging between the small men and the big outfits, C. E. was always standing up for justice, no matter for whom.

Butch Cassidy, individually, was not considered in the light of a rustler, through the annals of history or by his old time closer associates. Bank and train holdups were his specialty. Much could be said of the good side of a Bad Man, who down through many years of legend has been documented as the outlaw without a notch on his "Colt." But this is another story.

Mrs. Eldredge also stated that when he was working for her father, Butch gave her a mule when she was seven years old and helped her learn to ride it.

Butch's friends, John and Margaret Simpson, lived at Jakey's Fork on the Wind River, about five miles from Dubois, Wyoming. They were warm, hospitable people, and Butch found another home-away-from-home. Mrs. Simpson was a deeply religious woman and read the Bible every day. She reminded Butch of his own mother, and he felt very close to her. All his life Butch seemed to

Ida Simpson Redmond, about eighty-six years of age. She was ten when my brother began to spend a lot of time at the Simpson home. *Courtesy of Dorothy Hubbard.*

find a mother away from home, I think because of his great love for our mother; it furnished a temporary sense of security.

Mrs. Simpson could tell that Butch had also had religious training and knew he was basically a good man.[5] She would have been very lonely in that isolated area without Butch and Al Hainer. Mr. Simpson was away much of the time managing another large ranch, and "the boys" were always willing to help their gracious friend.

Dorothy Hubbard (granddaughter of the Simpsons) writes:

Mother [Ida Simpson Redmond] always has remembered the big beautiful Christmas Day they had in that log cabin. Butch brought them all things from Lander—some material for her a new dress and there were some neighbors there too. Grandma [Margaret Simpson] always had a wonderful garden with lettuce and celery that she had protected and all sorts of things, and canned it. And always had lots of jellies—buffalo berry, currant, gooseberry and even the wild strawberries. I was fourteen when she died and I remember well what a wonderful cook she was and what a great interesting person. Of course then I didn't realize what an interesting and dangerous life she had led and I wish now that I had written it all down.

Butch and Al were arrested and brought to trial for horse theft. From court records, it appears that there were two cases. A complaint dated July 15, 1892, charged George Cassidy and Albert Hainer with stealing one horse valued at forty dollars from the Grey Bull Cattle Company, organized under the laws of the State of New Jersey and doing business in Fremont County, Wyoming,

5. Letter from Dorothy Hubbard, daughter of Ida Simpson Redmond and granddaughter of John and Margaret Simpson, dated September 12, 1972. Ida Simpson Redmond lives with Dorothy Hubbard at the time of this writing and is well and alert mentally. She remembers Butch well, since she was about ten when he started coming to their home.

on or about October 1, 1891, in the county of Fremont, Wyoming. (An interesting observation is that the complaint came almost ten months after the alleged theft.) Later, a legal notice dated March 14, 1893, gave notice for George Cassidy to appear on June 12, 1893. Chas. Stough, Sheriff, served the papers. On June 22, 1893, the jury rendered a verdict of not guilty for both men. No other details were given of this case.

A second criminal complaint was brought before Charley Allen, justice of the peace, on June 19, 1893 (while the first case was in trial, apparently), charging George Cassidy and Al Hainer with stealing a horse valued at fifty dollars from Richard Ashworth on August 28, 1891. (Note that the date of this complaint is almost two years after the theft.) This constituted grand larceny. D. A. Preston and C. F. Rathbone appeared as attorneys for the defendants.

Both defendants were released on bail of $400. Will F. Simpson (a brother of John Simpson) signed the papers as county and prosecuting attorney of the County of Fremont in the State of Wyoming. The verdict was dated July 4, 1894:

We the jury find the above named defendant George Cassidy guilty of horse stealing, as charged in the information, and we find the value of the property stolen to be $5.00. And we find the above named defendant Al Hainer not guilty. And the jury recommend the said Cassidy to the mercy of the court. Geo. S. Russell, Forman.[6]

This is an actual quote from the court records, showing that while $50.00 is mentioned in one instance, $5.00 is mentioned in the other. Of course, I am not in any position to determine which is right. However, several times my brother expressed his bitterness for being sent to prison for the theft of a horse valued at $5.00. A motion

6. Fremont County Court Records.

was made for a new trial, but there is no evidence of such. Douglas Preston was Butch's lawyer.[7]

Before Butch was to be taken to the Wyoming State Penitentiary at Laramie to serve a sentence of two years, he asked permission to go and settle some business. He promised he would be back by midnight. He spent that time at the Simpson home. Then, true to his promise, he returned to be taken to prison.[8]

7. Douglas A. Preston, attorney for Butch Cassidy, enjoyed a long and colorful career as a successful politican as well as a barrister. After being educated in the public schools, he entered the law offices of his father Judge Finney D. Preston. He was admitted to the Illinois bar in 1878 and to the Wyoming bar nine years later.

From the time he became a resident of Wyoming in 1887, he was one of the leaders of the Democratic party and was a member of the state's constitutional convention. From 1903 until 1905 he served in the lower house of the state legislature. On January 3, 1911, he was appointed state attorney general by Governor Joseph M. Carey and four years later was reappointed to the office by Governor John B. Kendrick and served under both a Democratic and Republican Governor. He practiced law in Rawlins and Lander and opened his law office in Rock Springs in 1895. In 1928 he was elected to the state senate to fill the unexpired term of Senator Frank Yates.

In October, 1912, Preston married Ann Droullard. Anna was known as Peggy, his second wife. Very little was ever known of his first wife except that they had two children—a boy who died very young and a Mrs. Hugh Cox, who lived in Washington, Indiana, in 1929.

Preston was a brilliant criminal attorney, often outwitting his opponents with his surprise strategy. Pete Parker remembers him best from Pete's early days working in the drug store, Preston's seeming sternness concealing a chuckle. They were good friends until Preston's automobile accident which occurred on October 8, 1929, on his way home from Evanston, Wyoming. His wife, Peggy, was driving the car because Preston had never learned to drive. His injuries were not considered fatal, but he died of a heart attack; his obituary appeared in the *Rock Springs Rocket* on October 25, 1929, with the date of death listed as Sunday, October 20, 1929.

Although he was a great humanitarian and philanthropist, seldom were his acts of generosity known except by recipients. (Information supplied by Pete Parker.)

8. Letter from Dorothy Hubbard.

Old Lander Hotel, still in business although greatly remodeled. Butch stayed here. Since this picture was taken at the turn of the century, no doubt many of Butch's friends are in the picture. *Courtesy of Minnie Woodring.*

In later years, when people came to these families, digging up stories about Butch, they had little to say. To them he was tops. Rumors of his lawlessness found them to be unsympathetic listeners. The Simpson family always held it against Will Simpson for being responsible for his conviction. Mrs. Simpson insisted Roy Parker could do no wrong (and that's the name she knew him by). She never saw him after he was supposed to have returned from South America, but she knew Will Simpson caught a glimpse of him one day. Will stayed under cover, fearing reprisal.

In Rock Springs my brother was known as Roy Parker, so he must have used Cassidy and Parker interchangeably until after he got out of prison. It is also significant that the court records list him as George Cassidy (not Robert Parker), the same as the above complaints.

He was committed to the Wyoming State Penitentiary on July 15, 1894, as George "Butch" Cassidy. Of course, Pinkerton files also have this record, which accounts for the fact that writers have always referred to him under that inaccurate name. The name Butch Cassidy, by which he became known as an outlaw, could never link him to his family; and this was the way he wanted it.

Butch was a model prisoner. After a year and a half he appeared in the office of Governor W. A. Richards of Wyoming, by the governor's request. The Governor cleared his throat and said, "I'd like to talk to you."

"Go ahead, I've got all year," Butch replied.

"I can't keep you in jail any longer; my conscience won't let me. But I can't turn you loose either—my cattlemen friends won't let me. So I have a serious problem."

"I don't quite see it."

"You should be able to see it. If you were a cattleman in Wyoming at this particular time, would you want a young fellow with your talent for leadership running around loose—particularly if he was a 'little on the rustle'? I'm not a fool, Cassidy, and I know what a leader of men you could be, young as you are, and I know there are far too many men of your age running around loose, just needing a leader. Ordinarily, I would forget that I knew you were in jail, probably on a frame-up, and let it go at that. But I've watched you, and I figure you're far too much of a man to rot in jail. If I could figure out a way to insure Wyoming, I'd turn you out."

"What do you want me to do? Leave the country? I'd as soon stay in jail as not be able to come and go where and when I wanted to. If I'm going to be free, I'm going to be entirely free."

"I see what you mean," the Governor nodded. "All I want to know is whether or not you'll start right in to organize the Hole-in-the-Wall outfit, and clean out the cattlemen of the state of Wyoming."

"Oh, if that's all that's bothering you, I'll promise you never to bother a hoof of anything in the state as long as I live."

"That's all I want to know," the Governor answered. "But why such a willing agreement?"

"I've had a chance to think," Butch went on, "and I've come to the conclusion that stealing cows and horses is just too slow a way to get rich. When you want money, Governor, the place to go after it is where it is."

"And that is?"

"In banks, Governor, in banks!"

They both laughed. It was such a witty answer and full of such cold logic.

"Then how about including banks in your promise?"

Butch thought a long moment—Wyoming banks were very prosperous. Then he flashed his famous smile. "In your case, Governor, I'll include banks too. I'll let livestock and banks alone in the State of Wyoming."

He was pardoned by Governor W. A. Richards on these terms, and Butch often told the story in later years. He was released on January 19, 1896, and went directly to Brown's Park. But he was deeply bitter and had no intentions of going straight. He claimed he had been imprisoned on a trumped-up charge and that that prison term really made an outlaw of him.

My brother swore vengeance on Bob Calverly, who had arrested him at the time he was sent to prison. He threatened to rob A. C. Beckwith's Bank and Mercantile in

Two pictures of Lander, Fremont County seat; at top, 1885; at bottom, 1905. The pictures show Main Street and Lander's growth during the twenty-year period. *Courtesy of Minnie Woodring.*

Evanston and boasted that Bob couldn't catch him, either.

Upon hearing the rumor, Bob Calverly wrote to Butch, as follows:[9]

Butch: I've heard what you propose to do. Beck-with will not stand for it and neither will I. We will be waiting for you with every man in Evanston at our side. You can't hope to succeed and I hope you will reconsider what you propose to do. Let me know if you will talk it out. I will listen to what you have to say and will promise you no one will lay a hand on you if you come in alone. But if you come in armed and with friends we will be ready.

Bob Calverly

Butch replied:

Dear Bob: I got your note all okay. Had to see for myself. I have been in town had a drink and seen your defenses. You are a man of your word. But I had to see for myself. You have my promise that I won't bother your town again. But you have got to be more careful. I had my sights on you three times last night. Bob, if I would have been any other man you would have been a dead man this morning.

Butch Casidy

I wonder if my brother honestly believed it was this prison sentence that made an outlaw of him? Is it possible that prior to his sentence he had revived hopes of going straight?

9. These two letters are quoted as a courtesy of Kerry Ross Boren of the National Center for Outlaw and Lawmen History at Utah State University, Logan, Utah. He saw and copied the letters when they were in possession of Tom Welch, a mutual friend of Butch and of Bob Calverly.

Butch's prison photo. *Courtesy of Wyoming State Archives and Historical Department.*

Wyoming State Penitentiary

Post Office Box 400
Rawlins. Wyoming 82301

Ph. 307 324-4171

Lenard F. Meacham. Warden

August 31, 1973

Ms. Dora D. Flack
448 East 775 North
Bountiful, Utah 84010

Dear Ms. Flack:

In reply to your letter of August 21st, we are enclosing a copy of the photo taken of
George "Butch" Cassidy at the time of his incarceration and also a copy of the meager
information we have mimeographed concerning him to give out to the interested public.

The following information has been taken directly from the Bertillion Book which accom-
panied territorial prisoners from Laramie, Wyoming to Rawlins, Wyoming and is the sum
of our information concerning him:

Name: George "Butch" Cassidy; WSP #187; Rec'd. 7-15-1894; Crime, Grand Larceny;
County, Fremont; Sentence, Two (2) Years from 7-15-94; Age 27; Nativity, New York
City; Occupation, Cowboy; Height, 5'9"; Complexion, Light; Hair, Dark Flaxen; Eyes,
Blue; Wife, No; Parents, Not Known; Children, No; Religion, None; Habits of Life,
Intemperate; Education, Com. School; Relations Address, Not Known; Weight, 165#;
Marks, Scars: Features, regular, small deep set eyes, 2 cut scars on back of head,
small red scar under left eye, red mark on left side of back, small brown mole on calf
of left leg, good build; Discharged, 1-19-1896, Pardon Order W. A. Richards, conduct
good, N. D. McDonald, Warden.

Sincerely,

Duane Shillinger M.D.

Duane Shillinger
Administrative Assistant

DS/ms
Enclosures

(Above). Letter from Wyoming State Penitentiary.

**(Right). Information dated July 15, 1892, for a complaint charging
Cassidy and Hainer with stealing a horse valued at forty dollars. This
information was the beginning of case no. 144 — the State of
Wyoming vs. Cassidy and Hainer.**

THE STATE OF WYOMING, } ss.
COUNTY OF FREMONT.

In the District Court for said County.

INFORMATION.

Comes now *James S. Vidal*, County and Prosecuting Attorney of the County of Fremont, in the State of Wyoming, and in the name and by the authority of the State of Wyoming, informs the Court and gives the Court to understand that *George Cassidy* and *Albert Hainer*, late of the County aforesaid, on the *First* day of *October*, A. D. 189*1*, at the County of Fremont, in the State of Wyoming, did *One horse of the value of Forty Dollars, of the goods, chattels and personal property of the Grey Bull Cattle Company, a corporation duly organized and existing under, and by virtue of the laws of the State of New Jersey, and doing business within the said County of Fremont, State of Wyoming, unlawfully, knowingly and feloniously did steal, take and carry away, lead away, drive away and ride away;*

Contrary to the form of the Statute in such case made and provided, and against the peace and dignity of the State of Wyoming. *James S. Vidal,*

County and Prosecuting Attorney of the County of
Fremont, in the State of Wyoming.

THE STATE OF WYOMING, } ss.
COUNTY OF FREMONT.

I *James S. Vidal*, County and Prosecuting Attorney of the County of Fremont, in the State of Wyoming, do solemnly swear that I have read the above and foregoing information by me subscribed, that I know the contents thereof, and that ~~the facts therein stated are true~~ *I have been reliably informed and verily believe the facts therein stated are true;*

so help me God.

James S. Vidal,

Sworn to before me and signed in my presence this *15th* day of *July* A. D. 189*2* and I so hereby certify.

Ben Sheldon
Clk Dist Court
within and for Fremont
County, Wyoming.

101

Bail fixed at $400.00 each

No. 144 Ct. Judge

THE STATE OF WYOMING.

vs.

George Cassidy and Albert Hayner, Defendants.

INFORMATION:

Filed *Filed July 16th 189_*

B. F. Fowler

Defendant pleads Not Guilty

WITNESSES EXAMINED. *Otto Frau*

Prosecuting Witness,

Fred Stagner. James Thomas

David Blanchard. J. W. Chapman

David Stewart. Jos. A. Mitchno

James L. Vidal

County and Prosecuting Attorney
for Fremont County, Wyo.

of within Information

Certified Copy served
on defendants
July 16th A D 1892
at 9:15 a m

B. F. Sheldon

Document dated July 16, 1892, detailing case of Wyoming vs. Cassidy and Hainer (Hayner), no. 144.

102

The State of Wyoming }
County of Fremont } ss.   In District Court
                                3rd Judicial Dist.

Legal Notice.

To *Fred. A. Whitney*, A SURETY ON THE
RECOGNIZANCE OF *George Cassidy* WHO HAS BEEN
DULY BOUND OVER ON THE CHARGE OF *Grand Larceny*
TO APPEAR AT THE NEXT REGULAR TERM OF THE DISTRICT
COURT WITHIN AND FOR THE COUNTY OF FREMONT.
YOU ARE HEREBY NOTIFIED THAT THE NEXT REGULAR TERM OF
SAID COURT WILL BE HOLDEN AT LANDER, IN SAID COUNTY
BEGINNING ON THE 12TH DAY OF JUNE A.D. 1893, AT WHICH
TIME AND PLACE SAID *George Cassidy* IS REQUIRED
TO APPEAR OR A DEFAULT WILL BE ENTERED AGAINST YOU ON
SAID RECOGNIZANCE AND JUDGMENT RENDERED AGAINST YOU
ACCORDINGLY THEREON.

Witness my hand and the official
Seal of said Court this 14th
day of March A.D. 1893.

B. F. Fowler
Clk. Dist. Court

Legal notice dated March 14, 1893, requiring Butch's appearance at
court for grand larceny (case no. 144).

103

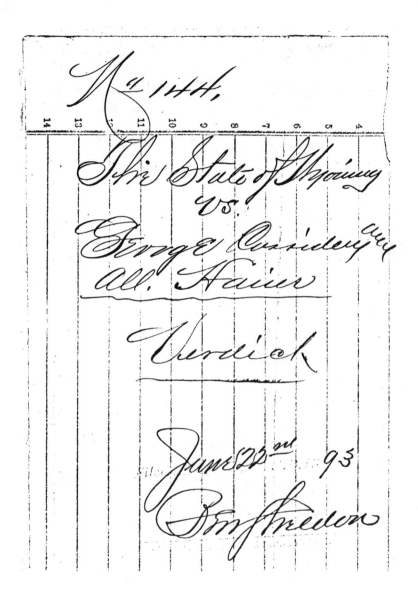

Cover sheet for the June, 1893, verdict of case no. 144 of Wyoming vs. Cassidy and Hainer.

The State of Wyoming
vs
George Cassiday and
Al Hayner

No 144

We the Jury find the above named defendants George Cassiday and Al Hayner not guilty

Seddon Jones Foreman

Official verdict of not guilty in the case of Wyoming vs. Cassidy and Hainer (Hayner), case no. 144.

THE STATE OF WYOMING, } SS.
COUNTY OF FREMONT.

In Justice Court.

Charley Allen
Justice of the Peace.

The State of Wyoming
vs.
George Cassidy & Al Hainer
(Defendants)

CRIMINAL COMPLAINT.

Otto Franc being duly sworn, on oath deposeth and says: That on or about the *28th* day of *August* A.D. 189*1*, in the _____ in the County of *Fremont* and State of Wyoming, the said *George Cassidy and Al Hainer* did willfully and maliciously *unlawfully and feloniously take, steal, ride away and drive away One Horse, then and there being property of the Personal Goods, Chattels and property of one Richard Ashworth of the value of Fifty Dollars* against the peace and dignity of the State of Wyoming and Contrary to the form of the statute in such case made and provided.

Signed: *Otto Franc*

Subscribed in my presence and sworn to before me this *Nineteenth* day of *June* A.D. 189*3*.

Charley Allen
Justice of the Peace.

Criminal complaint filed June 19, 1893, against Cassidy and Hainer for stealing a horse valued at fifty dollars.

Bail fixed at *400.⁰⁰ each*

Jim Knight
Judge.

No. *166*

THE STATE OF WYOMING

VS.

George Cassidy & Al Hainer

INFORMATION

FOR

Grand Larceny

A TRUE BILL

Filed *Nov 13th* 189*3*

Bm Sheldon
Clerk District Court.

Each

DEFENDANTS PLEADS

Not Guilty

WITNESSES EXAMINED

Dorr Stewart —
John Chapman —
Charles F. Green
Henry Sherrock
Geo. L. Downe
Wro. L. Simpson

County and Prosecuting Attorney for Fremont County, Wyoming.

GAZETTE PRINT, LANDER, WYO.

Case no. 166 and entered plea information dated November 13, 1893, against Cassidy and Hainer for stealing the fifty-dollar horse.

106

D. A. Preston's acceptance of service of information on case no. 166 (November 14, 1893).

The cover sheet for the verdict, July 4, 1894, in case no. 166.

The State of Wyoming
vs
George Cassidy & Al Hainer } No 166

We the Jury find the above named defendant George Cassidy guilty of horse stealing, as charged in the information, and we find the value of the property stolen to be $5.00 And we find the above named defendant Al, Hainer Not Guilty. And the jury recommend the said Cassidy to the mercy of the Court. Geo S. Russell
Forman

Verdict in case no. 166, finding Cassidy guilty, Hainer not guilty.

No 166

*In the District Court
of Fremont County*

State of Wyoming

vs.

George Cassidy

Motion for New Trial

July 7th 94

Ben Sheldon

D. A. Preston

atty for Defendant

D. A. Preston's motion, July 7, 1894, for a new trial on case no. 166.

Montpelier Bank Robbery
Chapter 9

According to one account,[1] Matt Warner was destitute and in prison in Vernal on a murder charge. His wife lay critically ill. Townspeople, seeing Butch and Elzy Lay in town, suspected them of planning to break Matt out of jail. So he was transferred to Ogden, Utah, for trial. Aware that Matt had killed in self-defense, Butch and Elzy hired D. A. Preston. Naturally, a fat fee was involved. This gave Butch and Elzy the incentive to really prove their outlaw wings. Why not pull a bank robbery on their own?

On August 13, 1896, on a hot afternoon Elzy and Butch walked into the Bank in Montpelier, Idaho, and surprised Gray, the bank cashier, and the few customers present. They commanded, "Put up your hands. Don't make a sound. This is a stickup!"

While Elzy stepped behind the cage and ordered the assistant cashier Mackintosh to put all the bills into a sack, Butch held his gun on the customers. The gold was quickly bagged. Mackintosh looked out the window and spotted a man holding horses—a third bandit, he surmised. It was Bob Meeks. The bank customers stood like statues, not wanting to call attention to their own possessions. But they needn't have worried, for Butch and Elzy never

---

1. Willard C. Hayden, "Butch Cassidy and the Great Montpelier Bank Robbery," *Idaho Yesterdays,* Vol. 15, No. 1, Spring, 1971, pp. 2-9.

robbed common people. They hated what they called the injustice of bankers and cattle barons who, they said, took from the little man and amassed wealth. While Butch covered the bank patrons with his gun, Elzy almost casually walked out the back door where Bob Meeks held the waiting horses. He tied the heavy gold and silver bags to the little sorrel's pack and slung the lighter sack of bills across his own cantle.

"Don't make a sound for ten minutes," Butch ordered his victims. He, too, walked out the door and mounted his horse, and the three, with the loaded pack mare trailing behind nonchalantly, trotted out of town. Butch, a natural-born actor, could have fooled anyone with his act. Once out of town, they broke into a dead run and headed up Montpelier Canyon. At Montpelier Pass, the outlaws switched to fresh mounts, previously stationed in the quaking aspens. The pursuing posse was no match for them and finally gave up the chase. This was the pattern followed in most of the robberies perpetrated by those who became known as the Wild Bunch: stationing fresh horses at intervals so that they could easily outdistance their pursuers. They were surprised to tally only $16,500, but gave an advance to Lawyer Preston for Matt's defense.

However, in the account of the Warner trial in the Ogden, Utah, newspaper, *The Standard*, Sept. 10, 1896, No. 295, Vol. 9, the *Salt Lake Herald* is quoted:

It is alleged that the bank was robbed by Cassidy and his gang to secure funds for Warner's defense and that one of the attorneys in the case had already received $1,000 of the bank money. . . . Attorney Preston is from Rock Springs . . . says that inference . . . is a malicious falsehood. . . . He received his fee before the Montpelier robbery occurred. He was not employed by Cassidy or any of the alleged Cassidy gang.

Said Preston, "I understand that a certain Iowa hawkshaw who, by the way, couldn't track an elephant in the snow, claims that there is a reward of $2,000 for Cassidy. If he will deposit $1,000 in any bank, payable to the sheriff of Weber County upon the delivery of Cassidy, he (Cassidy) will surrender to any officer that wants him. Cassidy can prove by reliable testimony that he was not nor could he have been at Montpelier at the time of the robbery. The truth is that Cassidy is not wanted anywhere by the authorities."

Such was the maze of information and misinformation sifting through to us about Bob. It was usually very confusing, and, of course, I have no way of straightening out his escapades which have been so widely published. Readers accept newspaper stories as factual in every detail, when many times they are not. Yet newspapers were our only source of information.

In Ogden, Matt was convicted and sentenced to five years in the Utah State Penitentiary. Butch visited Matt's wife and gave her money to live on while Matt was in prison.

After the Montpelier Bank robbery, Butch and Elzy went to work in Huntington, Utah, for Jens Nielson.

Bob Meeks, the third bank bandit, left and was later spotted in Cheyenne by a sharp-eyed railroad detective who selected him as a likely candidate for a botched-up Wyoming train robbery some time before. Meeks had an alibi for the train robbery charge, but that alibi placed him in Montpelier. The chain of evidence closed in on him. He was extradited to Idaho and was tried and convicted of the Montpelier Bank robbery. On September 7, 1897, he was sentenced to thirty-five years in the penitentiary in Boise under his given name, Henry Meeks.[2]

2. The Idaho State Correctional Institution of Boise, Idaho, recorded the following about Bob Meeks:

We had this gentleman incarcerated under the name of Henry Meeks received Bear Lake County, Idaho on Nov. 7, 1897 for

I don't know who served this term for Bob Meeks, but it is interesting to note that a man by that name was working in Wyoming several years after this event. Jose (a shortened form of Joseph) Betenson, who later became my husband, and my brother Eb were just young fellows when they went to Wyoming to work for B. F. Saunders with the sheep in 1903. They got pretty well acquainted with the foreman. Eb let him know he was Butch Cassidy's brother, and they talked quite a bit about it. One day at a shooting match, Eb hit the bull's-eye several times. That put the fear into the rest of the fellows. This really tickled Eb and Jose, because Eb was never a good shot—could hardly hit the broad side of a barn. He'd had a stroke of good luck, that was all.

The foreman then informed them that Bob Meeks was herding a bunch of sheep over the hill and that he was in hiding, but the foreman knew who he was. Eb wanted to meet him. Meeks sent word he would talk to Eb if he came alone and without a gun. Bob Meeks told Eb during their short visit that he didn't know Butch Cassidy, had never even seen him. I don't know whether or not this was a blind. But it plants doubt in your mind about the things you read. Eb said that the man he talked to (who was supposed to be Bob Meeks) was badly crippled.

the crime of Robbery sentenced to 35 years. He was 28 years old when received, born in Utah, occupation was a rancher. He was ht: 71 in.; comp: dark; hair: black; eyes: lt. hazel.

Mr. Meeks tried to escape from the penitentiary on two occasions. The first time on 12-24-01; however, was apprehended on 12-25-01. The second time was on 2-23-03 through the front gate; however, was shot in the left leg by the guard, and apprehended the same day. Later that leg was amputated at St. Alphonsus Hospital in Boise. As a result of this he was sentenced an additional 12 years for Escape. He was sent to an insane asylum by the probate court in Ada County on 4-22-03.

Mr. Meeks was finally released on 6-6-16.

Castle Gate Holdup
Chapter 10

Some time in the thirteen years Bob had been gone from home, he fell in with the Hole-in-the-Wall Gang and the Powder Springs Gang, although he doesn't seem to have been given any "credit" for any particular job. Much has been written about these gangs, and the newspapers frequently carried news of their exploits. Naturally, my knowledge of these happenings was dependent on the newspapers and what I have since read.

Harry Longabaugh, known as the Sundance Kid, had drifted into the area and joined the outlaws. He was a handsome man, quite tall and dark, and was a flashy dresser. An expert gunman, he had a quick, mean temper, and he was a killer.[1]

The winter of 1897, after working for Jens Nielson in Huntington, the gang stayed at Robbers' Roost, their impregnable stronghold in the rock country of Utah. In his *Last of the Bandit Riders*, Matt Warner gives a description of Robbers' Roost:

---

1. Information concerning Harry Longabaugh is taken from a tape of a lecture given in Ogden, Utah, on June 25, 1970, at the Weber County Library, by a man who claimed to be Harry Longabaugh, Jr. Dr. Grant Reeder, Bountiful, Utah, taped the lecture, and it was transcribed by Pearl Baker. Again I cannot vouch for its veracity, but it seems to have debunked many errors commonly printed. At the same time, however, he gives *mis*information about my brother. Therefore, I am left again to wonder what is true and what is not.

It is a wild country—regular painted-rock desert. The wildest kind of buttes and spires and cliffs rise above the level of the mesas, worn by wind and water into every kind of human and inhuman shape you can imagine, and every color from white through pinks and reds to brown. If you look down into the deep, dizzy canyons on the edges of the mesas, it's wilder and more savage than ever. In some places the top of a mesa is flat, bare sandstone rock for miles. Outlaws in flight would sometimes make for such places, and when they hit 'em their horses would leave no tracks an ordinary deputy could follow.

The outlaw element knew more than most officers about this country, where its scattered seeps and water holes was [sic], and where the hidden trails led up on top of the high plateaus. This made Robbers' Roost for years—especially from 1870 to 1895—the greatest outlaw hideout in the United States.[2]

There were cabin hideouts at different spots with a headquarters at Crow Seep. Large areas of fairly flat grazing land were scattered between the steep rock areas, affording grazing and watering room and spots where horses could be trained.

Curious about the hiding places of Butch and the gangs he ran with, I looked in file 1899-1900 of Governor Heber M. Wells (*Robbers Roost and Butch Cassidy, Criminals*) in the Utah State Archives.

Robbers Roost No. 1: 25 miles east of Hanksville, Wayne County, between Green River and the Dirty Devil; it is called Buhr's Ranch. Three miles from the water troughs. Nothing but a dugout in the mountain 16x12 feet, partly covered by dirt. A man named Meade lives there.

Robbers Roost No. 2: On the Mesi between Horseshoe Canyon and Dennis Canyon. Dennis Canyon

2. Warner and King, *Last of the Bandit Riders*, Caldwell, Idaho: Caxton Press, 1940), pp. 76-78.

Original cabins at one of the Robbers' Roost stations, taken in 1973.
Courtesy of E. Dixon Larson.

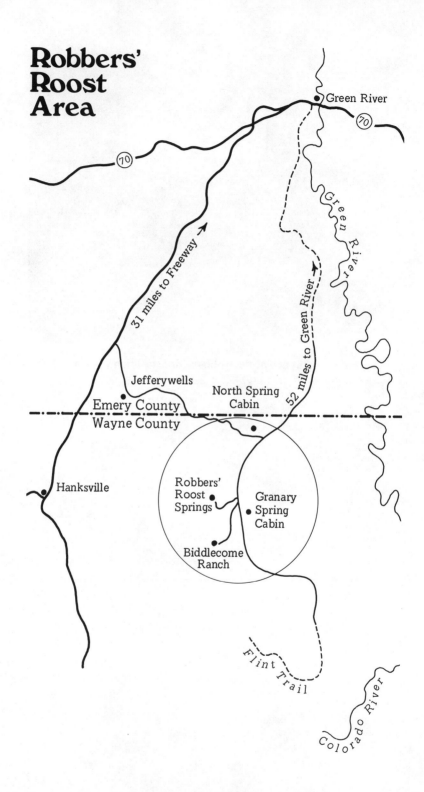

Robbers' Roost Area

Green River

70

70

31 miles to Freeway

52 miles to Green River

Green River

Jefferywells

Emery County

Wayne County

North Spring
Cabin

Hanksville

Robbers'
Roost
Springs

Granary
Spring
Cabin

Biddlecome
Ranch

Flint Trail

Colorado River

runs into the Green River. On the Mesi Cassidy, Lay and company reside. Had a tent 16x12. One place you have to jump the horses off ten feet into Dennis Canyon and the other places are at the head of Horseshoe Canyon and is difficult to get to.

Robbers Roost No. 3: Granite Ranch in the Henry Mountains at Buhr's place their residence on No. of Granite Wash. Seventeen miles southwest of Hanksville. Three log houses built jointly, having two windows on the south and the two doors on the north. Big cellar where they keep supplies. Corral right under bluff. Water supplied by a big spring just above the houses.

Robbers Roost No. 4: Known as Burts. Down Poison Springs Canyon twenty miles s.e. of Buhr's Ranch in a box canyon. Cabin 8x10 no doors.

Robbers Roost No. 6: San Rafael swale, about 20 miles from Castle Dale near Buckhorn Flats where the robbers passed through who robbed Carpenter.

Robbers Roost No. 7: East side of Colorado River about 15 miles below Dandy Crossing. Big Ring Cone. One cabin. On the trail that leads from the Colorado to Winslow, Arizona by the mouth of the San Juan River.

Elzy Lay had married Maude Davis, a lovely girl from Ashley Valley. A number of writers have cooked up an exciting story of Maude Davis and Ann Bassett swimming the Green River at night to a rendezvous on Diamond Mountain where Elzy and a "man of the cloth" waited. Reportedly, after the ceremony Elzy and Maude left on a honeymoon, and Ann and the clergyman swam back across the river. No one loved to tell a story more than Ann Bassett, and she has recorded this in her unpublished *Memoirs*. (Josie Bassett wrote of these memoirs: "better unpublished!") However, when Maude and Elzy's daughter, Marvel Lay Murdock, questioned her mother about this, Maude labeled it "ridiculous!"

Granite Ranch with Bull Mountain in background. The ranch house was built for J. B. Buhr when he ran cattle and horses at Robbers' Roost. Although this ranch is near the Henry Mountains, not at the Roost, it is where Buhr lived. Butch stayed here often. *Courtesy of Mrs. Mart (Edna) Robison, Hanksville, Utah.*

Maude spent the winter of 1896-97 with Elzy at Robbers' Roost. Etta Place, Sundance's girl friend, spent that winter there, too. A large tent was pitched for Elzy and Maude away from the quarters of the rest of the Bunch who were wintering there, and a second tent was pitched for Sundance and Etta. In her book, *The Wild Bunch at Robbers Roost*, Pearl Baker says that Butch and Etta Place stayed in this second tent. However, it is an accepted fact that Etta was Sundance's girl friend.

These outlaws all seemed to have one thing in common, and that was their respect for the other outlaw's woman. Since Sundance was so quick on the trigger, Butch would never have baited his mean temper; Butch had more sense than to play around with Sundance's girlfriend. Marvel Lay Murdock (the daughter of Maude Davis and Elzy Lay) has told me that she was not positive it was Etta Place who was there that winter. However, her mother often told her how beautiful Etta was, tall and stately, with raven dark hair, and she seemed to be a "lovely" woman. From the limited time Maude spent with Elzy, she probably would not have had much contact with Etta at any other time than that winter. Mrs. Murdock stated that she was sure the woman was there with Sundance, not with Butch.

In the spring, the camp was broken up, and the women returned to civilization. The Gang had spent the winter planning to rob the Pleasant Valley Coal Company in Castle Gate, Utah, of its payroll and training their horses for a clean getaway.

Railroad tracks wind through the bottom of the canyon where Castle Gate, a coal mining town, is situated. Many of the workers in the mine at that time were of foreign extraction. Twice a month the payroll was brought in on the railroad from Salt Lake City. Butch and Elzy had planned their exploit carefully to avoid any slip-up. Their horses had been disciplined and could be relied on completely. Butch practiced diligently until he could make a

Building housing the Pleasant Valley Coal Company, probably at about the time of the robbery, since one man holds a rifle. *Courtesy of the* Sun-Advocate *newspaper.*

running leap into the air and land squarely on a horse's back, and the horse was primed to take off on the instant of impact. Relays of horses had been prearranged at various ranches along the escape route to enable the outlaws to stay ahead of their pursuing posses until they could reach Robbers' Roost, sixty miles south of Price and beyond the law.

For a week they rode into Castle Gate and trained their horses so the train whistle wouldn't startle them. Our family read the account of the holdup in the newspapers.

The *Eastern Utah Advocate* of Price carried the story on Thursday, April 22, 1897, of the robbery committed the day before on April 21. The little town along the tracks was teeming with men waiting to pick up their pay. Butch and Elzy were inconspicuous in the group.

Elzy stayed on his horse, but Butch sat casually on a box by the foot of the outside stairway leading to the Pleasant Valley Coal Company offices. He leaned against the post, his light-colored slouch hat tipped over his eyes, presumably to protect them from the sun. He was dressed in denim overalls and a brown coat. At noon the D&RGW passenger train # 2 chugged into town.

The paymaster, E. L. Carpenter, padded down the steps in his houseslippers because his feet were giving him trouble. He hurried to the train with his deputy clerk and picked up two sacks of silver, one containing $1,000, the other $960, along with a satchel containing $7,000 in gold and another containing rolls and checks for $1,000—a total of $9,160.

Mr. Carpenter and his deputy clerk crossed over the tracks to the Wasatch Company's store and were just about to carry the money upstairs to the Pleasant Valley Coal offices on the east side of the building when Butch stepped in front of them. Poking his six-shooter into Carpenter's face, he said quietly, "Drop the sacks and hold up your hands." The astonished Carpenter complied. T. W. Lewis, the deputy clerk, ran into the store with his bag of $1,000 in silver.

The safe in the Pleasant Valley Coal Company's office at the time of the robbery. *Courtesy of the* Sun-Advocate *newspaper.*

Butch picked up the other two sacks and the satchel and tossed them to Elzy, who was on his horse, ready to make a quick getaway. Butch's horse shied away, and he spent some anxious moments getting control; then he mounted and sped off. The only effort to prevent their escape was a volley of three shots fired from the office as the bandits raced down the road. Everything happened so suddenly that the one hundred men lounging around waiting for the payroll were paralyzed.

Carpenter mounted the waiting engine. The train raced down the canyon after the highwaymen, the whistle screaming, but Carpenter couldn't see the horsemen anywhere. At Price the word spread like wildfire, and a posse was organized.

Butch and Elzy passed safely through the lower part of town and stopped to cut telephone wires. They left the sack containing $800 in silver by the road because it was too heavy. So they actually took with them $7,000 in gold. Posses were organized at Huntington, Castle Dale, and Cleveland to intercept the desperadoes. At 4:00 p.m. the mail carrier met them. They were four or five miles ahead of Sheriff Donant's posse, which left Price at 2:00 p.m. The mail carrier described the men as sun-browned and appearing like cowboys or common hoboes rather than desperate highwaymen.

No one followed Butch and Elzy into Robbers' Roost. Lawmen were not anxious to go into that area in pursuit because they realized the outlaws knew the terrain and lawmen did not. The newspaper described the country: "That country from Cedar Mountains on the east to Castle Valley to the Robbers' Roost in the Dirty Devil country is a continuous chain of upheavals. Its passes are narrow and precipitous and its streams are hundreds of feet below the mesas, running in chasms with perpendicular rock walls to hedge them in. The riverbeds are of

125

quicksand and altogether it is a perfect 'Dante's infernal region.' "

On May 6, 1897, the newspaper reported that ex-Sheriff Tom Lloyd and Pete Anderson returned from their futile hunt for the outlaws; the search was abandoned.

A year later, in May, 1898, Billy McGuire and Bud Whitmore were robbed, and the posses mounted again. According to the paper, Sheriff Allred's posse surprised a small group of men in a Robbers' Roost retreat. They opened fire, killing two outlaws and capturing two others. When the posse with the dead bandits and two prisoners arrived in Price, a large number of people gathered. The bodies were identified as Butch Cassidy and Joe Walker. They were prepared for burial on Saturday and were put in common wood coffins and buried on Sunday. However, "Butch's body" was exhumed the next day, and Doc Shores was positive it was not Butch. The controversy went back and forth until it was later determined that the dead man was John Herring.

When Butch learned through the speedy outlaw grapevine that he had been shot down, he couldn't resist the urge to view his own remains. Hidden in a covered wagon and looking through peepholes, he returned to Price. Butch watched the "mourners" and was surprised to see a number of women wiping their eyes. He was touched by such a display of emotion at his passing. Later he told us he had thought it would be a good idea to attend his own funeral just once during his lifetime. He told us, "No, it sure wasn't me. He was better looking."

The Castle Gate robbery had no Robin Hood motive; its proceeds would neither free a friend from prison nor avenge an injustice to a homesteader. It had been planned deliberately as a means of obtaining money for personal gain. Either my brother's conscience was hardening or his hopes for freeing himself from the outlaw life were dimming. Maybe both of these things were happening.

This picture was taken the payday after the robbery. Thirteen men hold rifles (shutting the barn door after the horses are gone). *Courtesy of the* Sun-Advocate *newspaper.*

The Wild Bunch
Chapter 11

The Wild Bunch (also called Butch Cassidy's Gang) kept the area stirred up. Most incidents of horse stealing, cattle rustling, or robbery were laid at their door. The Powder Springs Gang and the Hole-in-the-Wall Gang may have joined them. I do not know all these things for certain and must gather my conclusions from printed sources, not knowing where the writers got their information or how much is fact and how much is dreamed up. Correspondence in Governor Wells's files leads me to believe there was a lot of trouble then.

But I do have information I consider more reliable than most printed sources. Edna Robison is the daughter of Charley Gibbons, who kept the only hotel in Hanksville, Utah. She made a tape on September 28, 1970, that reveals very interesting first-hand knowledge about the Wild Bunch and particularly about my brother. The tape is in the possession of Marvel Lay Murdock of Heber City, Utah, who was present at the taping. I quote from it here:

These ladies have come for my story of the old Robbers' Roost days. I remember them well because they always came to stay at our hotel. My father, Charley Gibbons, had the only hotel and store and feed yard at that time. We always took care of all the boys who came. They were all wonderful people, Butch Cassidy especially, and Elzy Lay, and all those boys were just like cowboys coming in and staying overnight or maybe three or four days at a time, especially to rest their horses and get some good food. And we always enjoyed them. They never did any harm or abused anyone in this little village. My father was very well acquainted with them and even had letters from Butch Cassidy and the whereabouts of the boys after they left here. We always had a lot of respect for them.

I can testify that Kid Currie and Harvey Logan were two separate men, because they used to stay here with us and feed their horses, and we knew them very well. It has been confused that they were the same man, but they were not. They were two individuals. As I remember, Harvey Logan was quite a chubby man and heavy built and quiet, but you know, decent and nice acting. The other man Currie was on the same order, a little taller and real light, as I remember. They never made any trouble, so I think that they were pretty good bandits, as bandits go.

The boys came in one time. There was twelve, and our regular lunch was over with and so Butch came in the kitchen and asked Mother if she would get dinner for twelve. So she said to us little girls, "You take your dolls and get out of the way because we've got to hurry and get this dinner over with."

So we took our dolls and went upstairs, and we made a little pallet on the floor and laid down on the floor playing with our dolls, and my sister Dora went to sleep. Pretty soon when Mama called dinner, they all sat down at the table, and there was a wire in one of the extra chairs they had to use. Joe Walker sat down, and when his gun hit this wire it threw the gun around and it exploded. The trigger caught on the chair and it went right off and went up through the ceiling. Butch screamed, "My God, those girls are up there." And he was the first one upstairs to find out, and the bullet had spent and was lying about three inches from my sister's head. And he came down and said, "Don't one of you boys ever come in this house again with a loaded gun."

Another interesting story that I knew absolutely that it happened was Butch went into a place up the river here one time and found a lady alone, and she was crying,

(Top). Location of the Range Valley outfit belonging to Preston Nutter, about thirty-five miles north of Green River, Utah. Members of the Wild Bunch often stayed here. *Courtesy of John Grounds, Marysvale, Utah.*

(Bottom). Adobe Town, an area of rough country lying adjacent to Powder Mountain and Haystack Mountain hideout camps used by Butch's bands. *Courtesy of John Grounds, Marysvale, Utah.*

and he asked her if they had sickness or death or something, and she said, "No, we just got a letter that the person that holds a mortgage on this property will be here today to close us out, and we don't have a thing on earth except this little ranch."

And he said, "You just get me something to eat, and I'll fix it up."

She hurried around and got it on the table, something to eat; he was alone at that time. He asked how much they owed and she said, "Five hundred dollars."

So he went out to his saddlebags and got the $500 and said, "Now when that fellow comes, you act like you had just raised the money somewhere. He doesn't need to know where, and you give him that $500. But be sure you get a receipt and a release on this ranch."

She dried her eyes and she said she surely would. So after he had eaten, he went out and laid on the trail and knew this fellow would be coming horseback, so he laid on the trail and hid. So when this fellow come, he went out and held him up and took the money away from him. Her name was Mrs. Fred Noyes.

I might add another little incident that we were always fond of telling because Butch was such a fine young man to us. I had a sister just three years older than I. I was about eight and she was eleven. When the Bunch of boys would come into the yard, always with their guns, armed to the teeth, we didn't fear them at all. We just thought about getting out there and waiting for them and talking to them. Butch would always take us for a piggyback ride or a wheelbarrow ride or something. After supper was over, we would go into our little bedroom, and we would spread a Navajo rug and play jacks with ten- and twenty-dollar goldpieces and, of course, that was fun, and when we would get through playing and Mama told us to go to bed, why he would always give either a ten- or twenty-dollar goldpiece to us.

When he did come in, he would just tell the rest of the boys to take care of his horse because he was going to play with these little girls awhile. He acted like a brother that just come home. Then when they would have loot and bring the money in, they always gave it to my father, and he'd take it down the cellar.

There was no communication or transportation here other than just horseback or four- or six- or eight-horse outfits or freight wagons. There was nothing for him to do but do what they said. But they were always nice to him. And when they got ready for the money to take it and leave, my dad would give him the key and tell him to go help himself, and that's all that was done about it.

My father always told another story to show what a good boy Butch was. My mother had been making soap and left the cans of grease by the tub. Two or three mornings we got up and there was a coyote licking the grease out of the cans. Dad said, "If he comes tomorrow morning, I'm going to borrow Butch's gun, and I'll be ready for him." So the next morning when he got up, that coyote was licking those cans again. If he had shot through the screen, he would have likely got him, but then he tried to open the screen and the coyote got away. Dad said, "That was pretty trusting of Butch to give me the only gun he had on him." With the gun he could have held them all up if he had wanted to, but they were friendly and they never had any fear of each other.

Elzy Lay was a quiet fellow, but was always good and joined in with the others around the table. They never did have a conversation while we were there. They would come and rest their horses and stay three and four days at a time. We had some cots out under the trees, and we wondered why one fellow would go out and take a horse and go out toward Green River way on a high point and wait awhile to see if he could see someone coming. If he didn't, he would come back and maybe in an hour or two, maybe another fellow would go out and saddle his horse and go up to the west portion of the country to see if there was anyone coming. But we always wondered why it was and never knew until I grew older. The lawmen didn't want to meet them very bad. . . .

My dad said it was evident they didn't want to meet them here because it would have meant a shoot-out right here in the yard. The posse would wait until the boys *had gone, and then they came. They came and searched so many times to pick them up and finally a document of some kind came that if they would all surrender and come in and join .the Spanish-American war that they would release them, and that is when they went to South America. That is the last we ever saw of the boys. . . ."*

While the above information neither proves nor disproves Butch's involvement in particular robberies, it does affirm the high esteem in which many people held him. What a paradox my brother's actions were. Small wonder they have puzzled those of us who loved him.

The Outlaw Trail
Chapter 12

Butch's outlawry seemed to offer no turn-off at any point. He had to keep running, always staying just ahead of the lawmen, whose chase was relentless. He would have given anything if he could turn back and start life all over again. But "hindsight is always better than foresight," he reasoned. The friends he had chosen all along the way had kept him sinking lower and lower into the quagmire. They were all together in it. Was there no way to climb out? It seemed not.

At the ranch in Circleville, we learned through the grapevine and the newspaper of Butch's various escapades. My brother had promised Governor Richards of Wyoming that he would rob neither cattlemen nor banks in Wyoming, but his promise did not include trains.

We read that on June 2, 1899, the Overland Flyer of the Union Pacific Railroad was stopped by armed bandits near Wilcox, Wyoming; the robbery was laid at the feet of the Wild Bunch.

Charles Kelly gives a graphic description of the Wilcox robbery in his *Outlaw Trail*, which may or may not be completely true. At 2:18 a.m. the train was stopped between LeRoy and Wilcox, Wyoming, by two masked, armed bandits who ordered the engineer to uncouple the express car and move on across the bridge. After it moved a short distance up the track, the engine was stopped, and four more masked men appeared and began pounding on the express car. Messenger Woodcock refused to open up;

he turned out the lights and bolted the door. The outlaws exploded a charge of dynamite on the doorsill, blowing out the side of the car and knocking out Mr. Woodcock. Since the messenger could not give them the combination, they lit another charge of dynamite and blew off the safe door, completely wrecking the car.

Money flew into the air. The bandits escaped with what they could collect and made their getaway. Red-spotted paper money fragments were scattered all over the ground. Certainly someone's blood had been shed! The early light of dawn revealed that the money was spotted with raspberries instead of blood—the remainder of a box of raspberries in the express car.[1]

A number of train robberies seemed to fit into a particular pattern, and there is little doubt that Butch Cassidy and Elzy Lay masterminded them. Never were the passengers of the trains molested or robbed. The Wild Bunch was simply after the big money from the railroad and bank money being transported on the trains.

By that time Butch was using the WS Ranch near Alma, New Mexico, as his headquarters. In his *Recollections of A Western Ranchman, New Mexico 1883-1899*, Captain French tells of hiring Jim Lowe as a foreman on the WS Ranch in Alma. Jim Lowe was in reality Butch Cassidy. With Jim Lowe were two other men, William McGinnis (Elzy Lay) and Tom Capehart (Harvey Logan). Captain French noticed immediately that work on the Ranch took a decided turn for the better. Strangely, rustling from the WS Ranch came to a complete halt. When new men were needed, Jim always had someone available. Captain French marvelled at the way Lowe and

1. Charles Kelly, *The Outlaw Trail* (Salt Lake City: Charles Kelly, 1938), p. 241.

Express car blown up in holdup at Wilcox, Wyoming, on June 2, 1899. *Courtesy of Union Pacific Railroad.*

McGinnis handled the stock. With only a few cowboys they could take a large herd to the railroad two hundred miles away without losing one. French received reports that his hands were the best behaved of any who came into town, that their conduct was above reproach. Of course, French never suspected that he was harboring outlaws who were using the Ranch as a cover for planning train robberies at great distances. The "hands" came and went for "business reasons" but the ranch work was always properly cared for.

The Folsom Train robbery followed a month after the Wilcox—on July 11, 1899. In the subsequent chase and gunfire, two sheriffs were killed. William McGinnis (Elzy Lay), known as Mac, was falsely reported killed by the posse; he was seriously wounded. Subsequent events (see Appendix B) brought about his capture and sentencing to prison under the name of William McGinnis # PNM 1348 on Oct. 10, 1899, for a life term.

Since "McGinnis" was a model prisoner, the warden trusted him as his driver on business into Santa Fe. Reportedly on their way back from one of these business trips, they found the prison on fire and the warden's wife and daughters being held as hostages. Elzy persuaded the prisoners to give up and to surrender the women. Shortly after that event, on January 10, 1906, Governor Otero granted Lay a full pardon.[2]

While Elzy was serving his term, the circumstances of the Wild Bunch had changed greatly. Pinkertons had traced Butch to the WS Ranch; so Butch terminated his employment and headed for Arizona.

The Tipton Train Robbery occurred on August 29, 1900 (in the pattern of the Wild Bunch), at Tipton, Wyoming. Butch knew his time was running out and was eager to get money to skip the country. Detailed accounts of all these robberies are given by many writers, but because the details were not verified to me by my brother, Butch, I will not belabor them.

2. Harvey Lay Murdock interview, Salt Lake City, Utah.

Exterior and interior views of express car blown up by the Wild Bunch in a holdup at Tipton, Wyoming, August 29, 1900. *Courtesy of Union Pacific Railroad.*

The dust had hardly settled before the next job was being planned. This was to be the bank at Winnemucca, Nevada.

Mr. I. V. (Vic) Button has written several letters to me in which he supplies some interesting sidelights on the Winnemucca Bank robbery:

It was the fall of the year and time for the fall roundup. Cowboys came from Eden Valley, Grass Valley, Paradise Valley and Clover Valley. The roundup was held at the CS Ranch, a few miles east of Winnemucca on the Humboldt River, where I made my home.

About four miles down the river from the ranch-houses, three men had made their camp. I remember these men well and later learned they were Butch Cassidy, Sundance Kid and Bill Carver. Even though I was only ten years old I remember them clearly as this turned out to be quite an important event in my life. They had made their camp by a haystack. There was also a well where they could get drinking water. They were camped there for ten days. Each day I would ride down and visit with them. The reason I would go to their camp is because they had this white horse. I had never seen such a horse. He could jump over a willow fence, high sagebrush or anything. I rode a different horse down there every day. Butch would ride the white horse and I would ride the horse I had brought from the ranch that day but I could never beat the white horse. I told Butch that there were over a hundred saddle horses at the ranch but none of them could ever beat the white horse. He said, "You like that horse? Someday he will be yours."

I got pretty well acquainted with them. They would ride into Winnemucca every few days and bring back peppermint candy for me, [and] Dad would say, "I wonder where Vic goes every day?" My mother and me were the only ones that knew where I went. Of course we thought the strangers were just cowboys and the men at the ranch were so busy with the roundup that the men and their camp were unnoticed by them.

They would ask me all kinds of questions about

140

the bank. I told them there were three who worked there, Mr. Nixon, Mr. Lee and Fanny Harp. I told them all I knew about Mr. Nixon, and about Fanny Harp. I told them Mr. Lee was a "cranky guy." ... I also told them about "Soldier's Pass," a shortcut to Clover Valley.[3]

On September 19, 1900, the three cowboys made their way across the fields to town, cutting the fence in order to make a fast getaway into the hills. Butch and Sundance arrived first, and after a while Carver trudged along, looking like a tramp. He was dressed in hobnailed

3. Letter dated Dec. 1, 1970, from I. V. (Vic) Button of Sacramento, California.
    Another letter from Vic Button, Feb. 24, 1971, reveals an interesting sidelight:

> *... In the 1930's, when the banks had closed and were in the hands of the receivers, a man came to Winnemucca to work in the First National Bank as one of the receivers. During the time he was there a relative of his wife's passed away in New Mexico. They went to New Mexico to the funeral. When he returned he came to me with this story.*
> *He said that after the funeral, when they were at the cemetery, some of the relatives introduced him to some friends who had come to the funeral, mentioning that he had come from Winnemucca, Nevada. There was a woman putting flowers on a grave that was next to the plot where his wife's relative was buried. She came over to him and said she had overheard that he was from Winnemucca. She said the grave, where she was putting flowers, was the grave of her husband, and that he had been one of the three men of the Butch Cassidy gang that had robbed the Winnemucca bank in 1900. She asked if the "kid," Vic, was still there. She then said that of course he would be a man by now but that her husband had told her the story of how they had given him the horse. She also said her husband had come to New Mexico, changed his name, and they had lived a normal life. The bank receiver seemed sure she knew what she was talking about, otherwise how would she have known about the robbery, the horse, and even my name!*

Believing Butch and Sundance had never returned from South America, Mr. Button assumed the grave was Bill Carver's. However, since Bill Carver's death was in Texas (a well-documented fact, I've been told), Mr. Button now states this had to be Sundance's grave.

shoes and ragged clothing and carried a sloppy-looking roll of ragged blankets. What no one knew was that the roll of blankets concealed a ready gun. Carver was "insurance." He was to enter the bank and sit down to cover any unexpected emergency.

However, on the way to town Carver met a skunk, and in the ensuing battle, the skunk fired first. When Carver arrived at the bank, he couldn't stand himself. Butch and Sundance and the bank officials were nearly asphyxiated before the job was finished.

Hitting fresh air again, Butch dropped a sack of money and turned back for it; the bank employees began firing at him, but the wild bullets took out the windows of a nearby saloon instead.

Vic Button's letter continues:

After the robbery, Clover Valley is where three possemen caught up with them. They were Burns Colwell, Shorty Johnson and Jim McVey. Butch, Sundance and Bill Carver had opened and closed the wire gate and were changing their packs to fresh horses. They told the three possemen they would shoot it out with them. The possemen turned and rode back to town. This is when Butch shouted, "Give the white horse to the kid at the C.S. Ranch." It was at this point, when they changed mounts, that they left the white horse behind. We learned later that they had relay points set up every ten miles from their [sic] to the Idaho border where they would change to fresh horses.

Later the posse rode back to Golconda. Everyone was talking about the robbery. I was coming out of the schoolhouse. I looked up and there was my white horse. He was covered with lather from running so hard. I ran and jumped on him. Around the schoolyard was a willow fence and on the other side of the fence was a

Vic Button on the white horse given him by Butch Cassidy at the time of the Winnemucca bank robbery in 1900. This picture was taken nine years later when Vic was nineteen. *Courtesy of Vic Button.*

creek. First thing he jumped the fence and I rode him to the creek to get a drink. They all asked me about the bank robbers but all I could say was, "You see what they gave me." I gave him a name. I called him Patsy.

As I look back I remember these men were good to me. They seemed to have fun and joke amongst themselves. I can only say that for them to remember their promise to a kid when the posse was so close, that these men could not have been all bad.

I. V. Button.

In another letter that same year, Mr. Button added:

You will probably notice that I named posse members other than what you have read. Sheriff McDaid did not organize the posse. . . . I knew the posse members well, as they came to the school with the white horse.

Again Pinkertons were hot on the trail of the Wild Bunch. On the "wanted" bulletins posted for the Winnemucca holdup, they described Carver as having "a very determined face and smelling like a polecat."

The loot at Winnemucca was $31,000 in twenty-dollar goldpieces; $1,200 in five- and ten-dollar gold coins, and the balance in currency, including one fifty-dollar bill.

It is said that Butch wrote back to the bank, enclosing a picture of five members of the Wild Bunch—decked out in bowler derbies and the classiest of city-slicker duds—and thanking the bank for its contribution. (Some of my children and grandchildren have seen the picture on display in the bank.) Butch thought it was the least he could do—to thank them.

But that picture proved to be the downfall of those involved and put Pinkertons on the trail again. It placed them in Texas, where the picture was taken.

Even if the picture of my brother's face had been faded, I would have known him by his hands, for they were characteristic Parker hands, with long, tapering

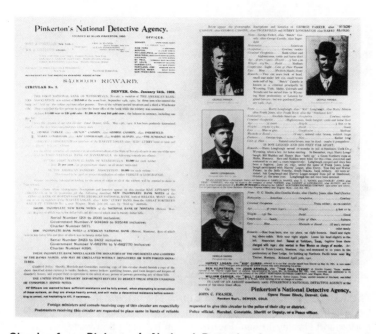

Circular from Pinkerton's National Detective Agency. *Courtesy of Sam Weller, Salt Lake City, Utah.*

The familiar picture of the Wild Bunch at Fort Worth. Sitting: Harry Longabaugh, Ben Kilpatrick, and Butch Cassidy. Standing: Bill Carver and Harvey Logan. Picture taken by John Schwartz, winter of 1900-01. *Courtesy of Union Pacific Railroad.*

fingers. Acquaintances have mentioned this marked similarity of the hands in that photo to my own.

With many characteristics similar to those of our family, Butch nevertheless pulled away and became a renegade. I have never ceased to wonder about that.

Pinkerton's National Detective Agency.

FOUNDED BY ALLAN PINKERTON, 1850.

ROBT. A. PINKERTON, New York, ⎫
WM. A. PINKERTON, Chicago, ⎬ Principals.

GEO. D. BANGS,
General Superintendent, New York.
ALLAN PINKERTON,
Asst. to Principals and Gen'l Supt.,
New York.

JOHN CORNISH, Ass't Gen'l Sup't., Eastern Division, New York.
EDWARD S. GAYLOR, Ass't Gen'l Sup't., Middle Division, Chicago.
JAMES McPARLAND, Ass't Gen'l Supt., Western Division, Denver.

Attorneys:—GUTHRIE, CRAVATH & HENDERSON,
New York.

TELEPHONE CONNECTION.

OFFICES.

DENVER, OPERA HOUSE BLOCK.
J. C. FRASER, Sup't.
NEW YORK. 57 BROADWAY.
BOSTON, 30 COURT STREET.
PHILADELPHIA, 441 CHESTNUT STREET.
MONTREAL, MERCHANTS BANK BUILDING.
CHICAGO, 201 FIFTH AVENUE.
ST. PAUL, GERMANIA BANK BUILDING.
ST. LOUIS, WAINWRIGHT BUILDING.
KANSAS CITY, 622 MAIN STREET.
PORTLAND, ORE. MARQUAM BLOCK.
SEATTLE, WASH. BAILEY BLOCK.
SAN FRANCISCO, CROCKER BUILDING.

Representing American Bankers Association.

$6,000 REWARD

THE FIRST NATIONAL BANK OF WINNEMUCCA, NEVADA, a member of THE AMERICAN BANKERS' ASSOCIATION, was robbed of $32,640 at the noon hour, September 19, 1900, by three men, who entered the bank and held up the cashier and four other persons. Two of the robbers carried revolvers and the third a Winchester rifle. They compelled the five persons to go into the inner office of the bank, where the robbery was committed.

At least $31,000 was in $20 gold coins; $1,200 in $5 and $10 gold coins; the balance in currency, including one $50 bill.

THE MEN WERE NOT MASKED AND CAN BE IDENTIFIED.

The robbers are described as follows:

No. 1 (who entered the cashier's office and forced him, under threats, to open the safe).

AGE, about 35.
HEIGHT, 5 ft., 9 or 10 in.
WEIGHT, 160 pounds.
EYES, blue or gray.
NOSE, fairly long, but thin.
COMPLEXION, light.
HAIR, light flaxen.

BEARD, full, flaxen or blonde, and moustache light weight.
HANDS, (No. 7 glove) very small and much freckled on backs.
FEET, small.
OCCUPATION, probably cowboy.

Remarks: Walked as if lame at the hip. This may have been assumed. Has small veins, which show quite distinctly on globe of cheeks.

No. 2.

AGE, about 35.
HEIGHT, 5 ft., 7 or 8 inches.
WEIGHT, 145 to 155 pounds.
BUILD, medium.

EYES, blue or brown.
HAIR, brown.
MOUSTACHE, moderately heavy, brown in color and drooping.

No. 3.

AGE, 25 to 30.
COMPLEXION, dark.
WEIGHT, 155 to 160 pounds.
BUILD, medium.

HEIGHT, 5 ft., 9 or 10 inches.
EYES, dark brown.
FACE, smooth.

Remarks: Very determined expression in face. Smelled like a polecat. Think his hair was colored for the occasion. Two of the bank employes say he had a scar on one side of cheek, something like a wrinkle or life line.

Wanted poster following Winnemucca Bank robbery. *Fremont County Courthouse, Lander, Wyoming.*

After a thorough investigation and from information received, GEORGE PARKER (right name) alias GEORGE CASSIDY, alias "BUTCH" CASSIDY, alias INGERFIELD; and HARRY LONGBAUGH, alias "KID" LONGBAUGH, alias HARRY ALONZO, are suspected of being two of the men engaged in this robbery.

"BUTCH" CASSIDY is known as a criminal principally in Wyoming, Utah, Idaho, Colorado and Nevada.

On July 15, 1894, he was sentenced to two years' imprisonment in the Wyoming penitentiary at Laramie, from Fremont county, for grand larceny, but was pardoned January 19, 1896.

HARRY LONGBAUGH, alias "Kid" Longbaugh, also known as Harry Alonzo, served 18 months in jail at Sundance, Cook county, Wyoming, when a boy, for horse stealing.

In December, 1892, Longbaugh, Bill Madden and Harry Bass held up a Great Northern train at Malta, Montana. Bass and Madden were tried for this crime, convicted and sentenced to prison for 10 and 14 years respectively.

HARRY LONGBAUGH escaped, and has been a fugitive from justice since.

On June 28, 1897, under the name of Frank Jones, Longbaugh participated with Harvey Logan, alias Curry, and Tom O'Day and Walter Putney, in the Belle Fourche (S. Dak.) bank robbery. All were arrested, but Longbaugh and Harvey Logan escaped from jail at Deadwood, October 31, 1897.

Governor Heber Wells (present governor) of Utah, in 1898, offered a reward of $500 for the arrest of "Butch" Cassidy for the robbery of Paymaster Carpenter of the Pleasant Valley Coal company, at Castle Gate, Utah, in 1897.

For the arrest, detention and surrender to an authorized officer of the State of Nevada of each or any of the men who robbed the First National Bank of Winnemucca as herein stated, the American Bankers' Association offers a reward of $1,000, to be paid upon identification of the prisoner or prisoners.

For the arrest, detention and surrender to an authorized officer of the State of Nevada of each or any of the men who robbed the First National Bank at Winnemucca as herein stated, that bank offers a reward of $1,000, to be paid upon identification of the prisoner or prisoners, and will in addition, in proportionate shares, pay 25 per cent of all money recovered.

Persons furnishing information leading to the arrest of either or all of the robbers will share in the reward.

In case of an arrest immediately notify **Pinkerton's National Detective Agency** at the nearest of the above listed offices.

PINKERTON'S NATIONAL DETECTIVE AGENCY,

Or J. C. FRASER, Resident Superintendent,   OPERA HOUSE BLOCK,
DENVER, COLORADO.   DENVER, COLO.

Denver, May 15th, 1901.

Bid for
Amnesty
Chapter 13

Butch was sickened by his outlaw life. Several of the Wild Bunch had already met violent deaths, and Elzy Lay was in prison. No decent end seemed in sight, and Butch certainly hadn't amassed any fortune for all his risks. Yet he hadn't killed anyone. Perhaps someone would give him a chance to go straight; he'd be better off financially to get a job and draw an ordinary salary. He knew the shame he had brought to his family—didn't even have the nerve to write home any more. At thirty-four years of age, surely he could still make a new life.

He approached Judge Orlando W. Powers in Salt Lake City and asked if there was any way he could be pardoned and retire from outlawry without going to prison. The judge doubted it. He couldn't be pardoned in Utah without having been convicted of a crime in that state. The Castle Gate holdup was the only crime of record on the books of Utah. Although he was given credit for it, it still couldn't be proven against him. And if he were to settle down, on a ranch for example, he would be besieged by justice demands from other states. Amnesty in one state wouldn't do him much good. Butch also consulted Utah's Governor Heber M. Wells.

It was necessary for him to be in Salt Lake City as he waited for word of the outcome of his pleas. While he was there, he became interested in a young girl. Ardythe Kennelly has written a charming book, *Good*

Dorney, Butch's one-time girlfriend in Salt Lake City. *Courtesy of Ardythe Kennelly.*

Morning, Young Lady, which she claims is a true story of this quaint love affair. Miss Kennelly has given me a picture of that girl, but I cannot use her real name.

After serious deliberation, Judge Powers was convinced that Butch was sincere in wanting to go straight. Why couldn't he be a guard on the railroad? After all, when the word was circulated that he was actually guarding the trains, no smart outlaw would attempt to rob them. Surely it would be the best insurance the railroad could buy. The fact that the railroad officials could see the sense in this plan and were willing to trust Butch speaks well for his character.

Arrangements were made for a meeting at Lost Soldier Pass on the Wyoming-Utah border in October of 1899.[1] Wary of a trap, Butch insisted that Douglas A. Preston be with them.

Butch waited hour after hour at the lonely cutoff. The silence closed in on him as he scanned the trail expectantly, and the wind now soughed gently through the trees, now swelled to a soft whistle. Clouds piled up overhead as a thousand doubts crowded his mind. At last he decided it was all a trick. What a fool they'd made of him! He scribbled a note on a scrap of paper and left it under a rock, informing his would-be employers he had waited all day, and they could "go to hell."

Sick at heart, he realized he had become a victim of his own mistakes that he could never rectify. He headed his horse down the mountainside in the other direction. What he never knew was that Preston and his companions had been delayed by a sudden storm and had reached the Pass twenty-four hours late. Someone discovered the scrawled note.

---

1. Kerry Ross Boren obtained this date from Agnes Wright Spring, who was secretary to Douglas Preston for many years.

Matt Warner was dispatched to find Butch so that misunderstandings could be ironed out. Although an outlaw's becoming a railroad guard sounds pretty far-fetched, it was no fairy tale and was a plan familiar to lawmen.

In his *Outlaw Trail*, Kelly indicates that Butch's bid for amnesty was refused by Governor Wells because the attorney-general had searched the records and had found Butch guilty of murder "in at least one instance."[2] Because Kelly got a good deal of his information twisted and does not detail time and dates, his conclusions are misleading in many instances.

Kelly explains that Matt Warner was dispatched to find Butch but that on the train the conductor handed him a telegram:

"All agreements off. Cassidy just held up a train at Tipton." Although this story leads one to believe that the events followed each other in rapid sequence, the situation was neither that simple nor clear.

The proposed rendezvous at Lost Soldier Pass was in October, 1899. Seven months later Governor Wells received the following letter:

May 30, 1900
Colorado Springs, Colo.

His Excellency H. M. Wells, Governor
Salt Lake City

Dear Sir: I desire to inform you that I have reliable information to the effect that if the authorities will let him alone and the UPRR officials will give him a job as guard, etc. the outlaw Butch Cassidy will lay down his arms, come in, give himself up, go to work and be a good peacable [sic] citizen hereafter.

---

2. Charles Kelly, *The Outlaw Trail* (Salt Lake City: Charles Kelly, 1938), pp. 270-72.

This might indicate that Cassidy is not far away and may have been near Thompson Springs last Saturday where the two sheriffs were shot to death.

> *Very truly yours,*
> *W. S. Seavey*
> *Genl Agent Thiel Detective Service*
> *P. O. Box 404, Denver, Colo.*

The intimation in this letter, rather than the Tipton train robbery, sealed Butch's doom with the railroad officials. The Tipton train robbery did not occur until August 29, 1900 (three months later); so it could not possibly have been the reason for squelching Butch's railroad-guard prospects.

Actually, in Governor Wells's correspondence is the following wire from William Preece (who was sheriff of Vernal):

Thompsons, Utah, May 27, 1900
Sheriff [Jesse] Tyler and Sam Jenkins were shot and killed by outlaws yesterday at 12 o'clock on Hill Creek about 50 miles from here. Notify Sheriff Allred at Price, Utah to come and bring 5 deputies with horses. Can you furnish 10 men and horses quick. William Preece, Sheriff

Posses from Moab, Thompsons, Vernal, and Price were organized and dispatched after the seven-man band of outlaws.

Sheriff Joe Bush heard of the incident two days later while waiting to sail from Seattle and wrote to the Governor:

"I think Tom Dilley did it and will be on the lookout for him."

He declared that he was sure he could have handled the situation at home much better than the other sheriffs had done.

The outlaws were pretty good at outwitting the

posses. Lawmen had a rough time of it, and yet they all wanted to get in the act.

From Grand Junction, Colorado, the Governor received this telegram:

June 1, 1900. Governor Wells: Have been two months on the trail men who killed Sheriff Tyler also others in Arizona I am paying own expenses. What is best for me to do. Edward Beeler,

Sheriff Apache County, Arizona

"Two months on the trail" seems to be a strange message when the wire is dated only four days after the killings.

On July 1, 1900, a wire came to the governor from E. W. Davis, mayor of Vernal:

Sheriff's posse from Thompsons afoot south of White River horses stolen. Expect Preece tonight.

There was no indication in the correspondence that my brother was one of those sought; but since he was labeled the leader of the Wild Bunch, he would be implicated even if he was nowhere in the area. According to other telegrams, lawmen were on the trail of the Powder Springs Gang, who may or may not have been the same outlaws.

By putting together the events that spread out over a ten-month period from October, 1899 (Lost Soldier Pass) to May 26, 1900 (the date of the killings of the two sheriffs), to August 29, 1900 (the Tipton Train Robbery), one can hardly give credence to Kelly's assertion that Butch had been found guilty of murder.

On July 3, 1901, a train robbery at Wagner, Montana, following the pattern of the Wild Bunch, pretty well closed their career in the United States. Included in the loot were unsigned bank notes being shipped by train for the National Bank at Helena and for the American Bank at Seattle, Washington. These unsigned notes later

The "post-office" tree at Linwood, Utah. Butch and others of the Wild Bunch used this tree as their post office, addressing a letter to a fellow gang member in care of Robbers' Roost. The next member of the Bunch who came along delivered the letter. The tree had a hole in it, wrapped around by an iron band. Inside the hole was a bottle with a string attached. Notes were put into the bottle and let down into the tree, after which the hole was plugged and the iron band replaced to conceal the plug. The tree was used from about 1896 to 1902. Originally much taller, it was sawed off sometime between 1908 and 1910. *Courtesy of Kerry Ross Boren, National Center for Outlaw and Lawmen History, Utah State University, Logan, Utah.*

A full shot of Butch's Winchester, shown earlier. The smooth butt substantiates Butch's title: "the outlaw without a notch in his gun." *Courtesy of Jim Earle.*

spelled the doom of some of the members of the Wild Bunch. But at the time, all the bandits escaped the hundred-man posse. Those reported to be involved in the robbery were Harvey Logan, "Deaf Charley" Hanks, Butch, and Sundance who, this time, rode as a paying passenger.[3]

On July 7, 1903, another train robbery occurred near Parachute, Colorado, again similar to the others and again credited to the Wild Bunch. Since Butch and Sundance were in South America at the time, however, they could not have been involved in the robbery.[4]

One desperado was shot, but the others escaped. As the posse closed in on the wounded man, they heard one shot and found a dead bandit. He was at first identified as Lowell Spence but was later exhumed and "positively identified as Harvey Logan."[5] In 1949 Lowell Spence was still living.

Such were the questionable identifications that were made in several instances. Perhaps authorities were so eager to rid their files of an outlaw that they jumped to quick conclusions. I have been in touch with an informant who swears Harvey Logan was with Butch and Sundance in South America.

But whatever robberies he had been responsible for, Butch wanted out. To show his intent to go straight, E. Dixon Larson tells me, Butch turned in two guns to Sheriff Parley Christensen of Levan: A Colt .45 single-action revolver, serial # 158402, made in 1895. According

3. James D. Horan, *Desperate Men* (New York: Doubleday & Co.), pp. 243-44.

4. James D. Horan and Paul Sann, *Pictorial History of the Wild West* (New York: Crown Publishers, Inc.), p. 218. It is interesting to note that in his *Pictorial History of the Wild West*, Horan claims that Butch, Sundance, and Etta left for South America on February 20, 1901; yet in *Desperate Men* he claims they participated in the Parachute Robbery (1903). Such are the printed contradictions even by the same author.

5. Kelly, p. 286.

to his search with the manufacturer, it was shipped early in that year from the Colt Factory to J. F. Schmeizer, a large wholesaler of firearms in Leavenworth, Kansas. It was then shipped to the Ashley Co-op in Vernal. This would have been in the late 1890s. As nearly as Larson can trace it, Butch bought the gun in Vernal in 1896 and kept it until late in 1899 when he reportedly turned it in with a Winchester 73 44-40 Saddle Ring Carbine, Serial # 64876.

To South America
Chapter 14

As I said previously, the picture taken in Texas was a foolhardy gesture. I guess their sense of humor got the best of them at that point, but it turned out to be a real lead for Pinkertons, pinpointing their location. So the members of the Bunch, who were living high in Texas, knew it was time to go separate ways. Butch and Sundance decided to make good their plan to leave for South America. The two separated, arranging to meet in New York to sail from there. When they met in New York, however, Sundance had Etta Place with him and insisted that she go along.

At first Butch objected. South America was no place to take a woman, he said. But after serious consideration, he decided that if they were going straight down there, they surely needed a good cook and housekeeper. Etta was an extremely beautiful woman and usually dressed in black, setting off her elegance. According to most writers, the trio rented rooms in New York and decided to see the sights for a couple of weeks. They dressed like millionaires and spent money freely on shows, dinners, and seeing the sights.

Butch, Sundance, and Etta Place reportedly embarked for South America in 1901. Upon arriving in Buenos Aires they went to the government land office where they filed application for land. They received "four square leagues" in Cholilo, Province of Chubut, on October 16, 1901.

I cannot verify the above information, but I do know they were ranching in Cholilo by August, 1902, through a letter written by Butch to the mother of Maude Davis Lay dated August 10, 1902. The letter gives a picture of their life in Argentina. Unfortunately, it is not complete and lacks Butch's signature. However, Marvel Lay Murdock (Maude and Elzy Lay's daughter) has had this part of the letter for many, many years, and another family member had the last page with the signature. When they decided the letter should be housed in the Utah State Historical Society, the second half (bearing the signature) had disappeared. But Mrs. Murdock has remembered the letter all her life as a valuable family possession and that it was, in very fact, a letter from Butch. This was attested to her by both her mother (Maude Davis Lay) and her grandmother (Mrs. Davis of Ashley) to whom the letter is addressed.

A photostat of the letter appears here to show Butch's handwriting, which resembles my grandfather Parker's. Unfortunately, Scotch tape was used to hold the letter together instead of permitting it to break at the folds, and it is difficult to see those sections. So a typescript is also given for clarity.

Cholila, Ten Chubut
Argentina Republic S. Am.
August 10, 1902

Mrs. Davis
Ashley, Utah

My Dear Friend.
I suppose you have thought long before this that I had forgotten you (or was dead) but my dear friend, I am still alive. And when I think of my Old friends you are always the first to come to my mind. It will probably surprise you to hear from me away down in this country but U.S. was to small for me the last two years I was there. I was restless. I wanted to see more of the world. I had seen all of the U.S. that I thought was good. And a few

162

months after I sent A—— over to see you, and get the Photo of the rope jumping of which I have got here and often look at and wish I could see the originals, and I think I could liven some of the characters up a little for Maude looks very sad to me.

Another of my Uncles died and left $30,000 Thirty Thousand to our little family of 3 so I took my $10,000 and started to see a little more of the world. I visited the best Cities and best parts of the countrys of South A. till I got here. And this part of the country looked so good that I located, and I think for good, for I like the place better every day. I have 300 cattle, 1500 sheep, and 28 good saddle horses, 2 men to do my work, also good 4 room house, wearhouse, stable, chicken house and some chickens. The only thing lacking is a cook, for I am still living in Single Cussidness and I sometimes feel very lonely for I am alone all day, and my neighbors don't amount to anything, besides the only language spoken in this country is Spanish, and I don't speak it well enough to converse on the latest scandals so dear to [?] hearts of all nations, and without which conversations are very stale. but the country is first class. The only industry at present is stock raising (that is in this part) and it cant be beat for that purpose. for I never seen a finer grass country, and lots of it hundreds and hundreds of miles that is unsettled and comparatively unknown, and where I am it is a good agricultural country, all kind of small grain and vegetables grow without Irrigation but I am at the foot of the Andes Mountains. And all the land east of here is prarie and deserts, very good for stock, but for farming it would have to be irrigated, but there is plenty of good land along the mountains for all the people that will be here for the next hundred years, for I am a long way from civilization. It is 16 hundred miles to Buenos Aires the Capitol of the Argentine, and over 400 miles to the nearest RailRoad or Sea Port in the Argentine Republic but only about 150 miles to the Pacific Coast. [The corner of the page was torn off.] Chile but to get there we have to cross the mountains which was thought impossible last summer when it was found that the Chilian Gov. had cut a road *almost across so that next summer we will be able to go to Port Mont, Chile in about 4 days, where it used to take 2 months around the old trail and it will be a great benefit to us for Chile is our Beef market and we can get our cattle there in 1/10 [?] the time and have them fat. And we can also [illegible] supplies in Chile for one third of what they cost here. The climate here is a great deal milder than Ashley Valley. The Summers are beautiful, never as warm as there. And grass knee high every where and lots of good cold mountain water. but the winters are very wet and disagreeable, for it rains most of the time, but sometimes we have lots of snow. but it dont last long, for it never gets cold enough to freeze much. I have never seen Ice one inch thick."*

    from Butch Casidy George Parker [added in different handwriting]

Many outlaws were operating in South America and copied patterns of thefts committed by members of the Wild Bunch in the United States. So once again Butch was given much credit that wasn't due him. Butch realized there was no way out as long as he was alive; he was in too deep to climb out. Many ideas and events concerning their activities in South America have been related; again I cannot verify them. Possibly, Butch did his share. Occasionally we heard of or read accounts which led us to believe he was on the "trail" again.

Mother's heart was broken over this wayward son. Her prayers remained unanswered. Even though we were a fun-loving lot, always there was the undercurrent of shame and humiliation. But Mother continued to teach her church classes. No one knew the burden she carried. She suffered occasional severe sick spells.

One day Mother had been over helping my cousin with some sewing. We could see her coming through the field toward home. (We were living in the brick house in town by then.) Suddenly she stopped, rigid in her tracks. As she stood, unmoving, we knew something was wrong. When we reached her, she couldn't walk.

Dad took her to Panguitch because there was no doctor in Circleville. But although there was a doctor in

Cholila, Ter Chubut
Argentine Republic S. Am.
August 10, 1902

Mrs. Davis
Ashley, Utah

My Dear Friend.

I suppose you will have thought long before this that I had forgotten you...

Photocopy of letter written by Butch, now in possession of Utah Historical Society. Creasing and taping the letter have rendered it nearly illegible. *Courtesy of Harvey L. Murdock.*

Our mother, Annie Gillies Parker at about forty-eight years of age.

Panguitch, there was no hospital there (nor anywhere in our part of the state). So the doctor put her in a room in the hotel run by Mrs. Crosby, where he could watch her closely. She was there for three weeks. I was the oldest unmarried girl at home (twenty-one at the time), so I went to the hotel to care for Mother. Dad and I did all we could, but she grew weaker and weaker. It was her heart. The doctor could do nothing for her, but we refused to give up hope until she slipped away peacefully on May 1, 1905, with Dad and me at her side.

The people in Panguitch made her burial clothes. They were all so kind to us. We took her body home to Circleville in a buggy on a chilly, windy day, and the family met us in Circleville Canyon. Her viewing was held in our brick home in town. In those days we had no undertaker; so we kept fruit bottles filled with ice around her body until she was buried. Hers was the first funeral service held in the new rock schoolhouse that later burned down. She was buried in the Circleville Cemetery on a slight elevation to the north of town, a serene, quiet spot, offering a view of the whole valley.

Mountains surrounded us in all directions, and we seemed to gain strength from those "hills of home." The broad valley, nestled within the circle of those heights, spread out before us in cultivated squares of varying shades of spring green with brown patches waiting to be planted. There were large areas of uncultivated sagebrush. These fields and meadows extended to the east and blended with the juniper-studded foothills. We felt a measure of comfort as we stood beside the coffin. Then it was lowered into the ground and, even though I am ninety years old, to this day I can hear the shovels of dirt thudding on top of that box. Death seemed a lot worse in those days.

Mother's death was a great shock to the whole family. She had always made the best of things and looked on the bright side, and we couldn't reconcile ourselves to being without her at first. We lacked the great faith she possessed. For many days Dad walked all the way out to the ranch and back to wear out his grief.

Many times, when I heard my brother Eb walking in the night, unable to sleep, I slipped out of bed, and we walked to the cemetery and sat beside her grave and talked. The moonlight often bathed the whole valley in a soft, quiet glow. From the serenity of that spot, we gained inner strength.

Late one morning, Eb stopped at the house. His eyes were swollen and red, and I knew he'd been to the cemetery. He smiled and straightened to his full height, as he said, "It's all right now, Cute. I've been up to the cemetery for a long time, and I think I've had it out with myself." After that, he was better and able to face life without Mother.

Mother was only fifty-eight when she died, and I have always felt she literally died of a broken heart.

A number of writers have claimed my brother returned for Mother's funeral. One author whom I know personally leaves his readers with the impression that I told him my mother lay in state in Circleville for twenty-four hours with no visitors and that Butch paid his respects that night. This is not true. We had an almost continuous flow of friends and relatives until time for the funeral on May 5. Butch, in South America, did not even know of Mother's death, and he certainly did not come. I was there all the time. Julia Robinson and Vinnie Applegate came in and took over, cooking the meals and doing everything possible to ease our grief.

I am sure Bob always figured he was living his own life. He didn't realize that when he went to prison, a whole family was sentenced with him, especially Mother and Dad. Even though he escaped retribution so many times by evading the law, we felt the full impact of his crimes. No amount of rationalizing that he was a Robin Hood—taking from the rich and giving to the poor—could relieve our parents of the terrible load they carried every day of their lives because of him.

I think Sundance and Etta were on their own for a while in South America, as Butch was, as indicated in his letter to Mrs. Davis. But later the three had a ranch together.

Because Butch and Sundance were recognized in South America, they had to move northward into the mining areas, where they obtained work. One evening Sundance dropped a boastful hint that he and Butch were the outlaws who were causing uncertain relations between some of the South American countries and the United States. Sundance drank a good deal, and his tongue was often in a slick place. Butch was furious over these slips of the tongue. Just when things were going smoothly, he had to settle accounts with the mining company and leave, much to his disappointment.

Sundance had rather an ugly disposition and was morose and moody, while Butch got along with everyone, was generous with the natives, and carried sweets in his pockets for the kids. Consequently, when investigators went into an area, information about him was hard to get. He later told us that the lawmen really weren't interested in arresting him. On one occasion, after a holdup, he met the sheriff on a narrow trail; they greeted each other, and the sheriff went on his way without trying to make an arrest.

Butch also told us of one job he "cased" but never pulled off. He went to the Huanuni mines in Bolivia to look over the prospects of a payroll robbery. According to his custom, he posed as a prospector down on his luck and was invited in and treated royally. Afterward he refused to rob those men who had treated him so well.

Etta Place became ill and had to return to the United States for medical attention. Sundance and Butch came with her. Apparently they still had holdings in some of their previous outposts, because Cowboy Joe, a colorful character, has written to me that as a boy he was a horse wrangler for Butch and Sundance from 1906 to 1908.

In a letter dated May 16, 1972, he tells some of his impressions of Butch:

Butch Cassidy was born in a Christian atmosphere. I too was born of a Christian family. And when I told my tale of woe to Butch as to how my grandmother washed my neck and ears early Sunday morning and took me to Sunday School, made me stay for church, back for Epistle League and then church again Sunday evenings, plus a week-night meeting, my tale of woe, father running

*away from home, got me nowhere with Butch. He darn
quickly informed me that what I needed was more of the
same and the toe of a dad's boot lifting my fanny. And
that had I not come from a broken home my dad may
have seen that I didn't acquire the desire to run away from
home. . . .*

> *He volunteered to take me into Rock Springs
and have Etta put me on the train and send me back to my
mother. Etta was Harry Longbaugh's sweetheart, you must
know beyond all doubt. They planned some day to retire
from the owl hoot trail and settle down somewhere in the
deep south near some of Etta's kin folks. It got to be a
joke among those rough and daring men, that some day
the Sundance Kid would climb into overhalls, heavy
rubber boots, a sloppy cap, and make his daily bread by
slopping pigs, to wind up raising a little family with Etta.*

In yet another letter he tells of my brother's
memories of home:

> *Butch's family will perhaps never know of his
great love for them, but I do. Remember I was his horse
gingler, and often he came out and talked to me evenings
when putting the horses on good grass for the night, that
they might be contented. . . . He told me how he sent
home a name for his baby sister one time. . . . Butch was
so hurt to think he had been framed and sent to prison on
that trumped up horse stealing count in 93, that he all but
choked with emotion when talking of it.*

> *. . . Butch had but one face and talked with just
one tongue.*

My friend Pete Parker has also furnished evidence that Butch was in the United States about that time.
Pete is the son of Harry Parker, who was errand boy between Butch and Douglas Preston in Rock Springs.

> *The last time Dad was on his way to college at
Logan, Utah, after the Christmas vacation, he and a friend
had to wait over night at the hotel in Ogden to get their
train for Logan next morning. (I have a letter from my*

170

aunt written to Dad while he was in school that winter and it bears the postmark of 1906.) There was a man sitting in the lobby whom he recognized. The man talked to Dad for half an hour or forty-five minutes and he asked all about his parents and certain other people in Rock Springs. The next morning when they got up to pay their bill, the clerk told Dad their room and breakfast had been paid for. A package with two white shirts was on the counter for Dad and in the buttoned pocket was a $20 goldpiece. Of course it was Butch Cassidy. I guess he thought Dad looked a bit shabby, being a student.

These two incidents are evidence that Butch did return, but he didn't come home at that time.

Butch and Sundance both went back to South America where they worked for the Concordia Tin Mines. When Clement Rolla Glass, the manager of the mine, hired Butch, he asked his name.

Butch replied, "Santiago Maxwell."

A few days later Sundance rode up the path to the tin mine on a mule, asking for a job, and gave his name as Brown. The two became reliable employees; Butch was even trusted with the payroll, even though the bosses learned who they really were.

Percy Seibert was also a boss at Concordia. He became very well acquainted with Butch in 1908. Whenever Butch visited Mr. Seibert in his sitting room, he always sat on a small sofa between two windows. This gave him a survey of three windows and the door, thus protecting his back. He was always armed with a frontier model .44 Colt which was inconspicuously stuck in his belt. Mr. Seibert said he never saw him under the influence of liquor except once, and Butch was most ashamed of himself because he couldn't walk straight.

Mr. Seibert found Butch to be a gentleman quite at home in the best of society. He was trustworthy in his dealings with mine managers as well as with the employees.

In South America Butch used several aliases: Santiago Maxwell, Jim Lowe, Mr. Ryan, and others. The Indians called him Senor Don Max. Some of the robberies committed by Butch and Sundance in South America are detailed in books; but again I make no attempt to verify or contradict the accounts.[1] However, I do know from Butch's own words that they were not responsible for all they were accused of. Other pairs and gangs of outlaws copied their methods in South America as they did in the United States.

I understand that in 1909 Butch and Sundance left the Concordia Tin Mines.

Then word reached us that Butch Cassidy and the Sundance Kid had been killed in a gun battle in South America. We were shocked and sickened. I am glad Mother was not alive to endure the hurt. Townspeople in Circleville were very kind and never mentioned it once to any of us. I never heard of one of our family who was twitted about Butch during all the long, sad years.

We doubted the stories; yet we feared they might have some foundation, and we were sick that Butch had supposedly added murder to his list of crimes. But what could we do but try to live normally?

Pinkertons claimed Butch and Sundance had been killed in the gun battle in San Vicente. When they had learned the pair had gone to South America, Pinkertons sent Frank DiMaio and Charley Sirringo after them. They trailed Butch and Sundance, losing them in Buenos Aires but locating them again in the Chubut Valley, where the detectives gave up the chase because the area was so inaccessible.

Kerry Ross Boren has proven without a doubt that the reported gun battle at San Vicente in 1909 had not occurred. However, in 1911 there was a gun battle at Mercedes, Uruguay, where two outlaws were killed. A

---

1. Events at the Tin Mines have been chronicled by both Kelly and Horan and hence other writers.

salesman from the United States was in his hotel room in Mercedes and overheard a soldier say, "Come down and see the dead Americanos bandittos." The salesman went down and was convinced the outlaws were Butch and Sundance. A year later he returned to the United States and went to see Frank DiMaio, to whom he told his story and assured DiMaio the dead men were Butch and Sundance. On this flimsy evidence, the file was closed.[2]

2. Kerry Ross Boren, a recognized authority on outlaw history, National Center for Outlaw and Lawman History, Utah State University, Logan, Utah.

Butch Comes Home
Chapter 15

After Mother's death in 1905, Father lived in the brick house in town with his six unmarried children. Since I was the eldest daughter living at home, it was my responsibility to try to keep things together. I am the only one of the girls who stayed in Circleville, and I remained very close to Dad and my brothers.

On New Year's Eve, 1907, I married Joseph Betenson, and we lived in Circleville, where five children were born to us: Pauline, Scott, Mark, John, and Barbara.

Most of the time my brothers were out on the range with the livestock, spending the summers on the mountain and the winters at home, feeding cattle and horses at the ranch south of Circleville. My brothers worked elsewhere as time permitted, but they helped Dad at the ranch also. They had always raised good horses, cattle, and sheep, but were only moderate stockmen.

One day, Jim Gass, a Circleville neighbor, came home from a trip to California and told me he had seen Bob getting on a train in Los Angeles. He and Bob waved to each other, but the train pulled out before they could speak to each other.

Jim had been a close friend of Bob's when they were boys. He told me of an incident when he and Bob were in the hills together, and a deer jumped out and refused to run away. They rode back and discovered a fawn lying on the ground, pinned down by a log that had

The old Parker home in Circleville, Utah, now overgrown and unin-habited. The left jog is where the porch and the kitchen door were. Our father sat there when Butch returned. *Courtesy of A. LeGrand Flack.*

rolled onto its leg. Jim said, "We'd better shoot it to get it out of its misery."

But Bob said, "No, we'll fix that leg." They dismounted, and Bob took a buckskin string, splinted the leg, tied the string, and turned the fawn loose. A master with knots, Bob did this so skillfully that, as the leg healed, the movements of the deer would wear it off. Jim had always said, "Bob couldn't kill a dog, let alone a man."

Jim also told me that Bob was a true conservationist. He said that in the fall of the year Bob always filled his pockets with seeds of wildflowers, and as he rode along on his horse, he scattered the seeds in barren places along the road or trail.

As we pursued our very ordinary lives, occasionally a rumor reached us that Butch Cassidy was still alive and had been seen in various localities. Dad seemed so sure that he was still living. We wondered how much he really knew. But if Butch ever communicated with Dad, we didn't know it.

One day in 1925 (I know it was in the fall just before school started) some of my brothers were out on the range with the stock. My brother Mark was fixing the fence at the ranch when a new black Ford drove up, and a man got out. It was a touring car—the kind with the old isinglass shades that you snapped on in a rainstorm. Mark looked up and surmised it was a cousin, Fred Levi. The Levi boys were cattle buyers, and Mark supposed he was coming for that purpose. The man walked across the field toward Mark. As he came near, his face broke into a characteristic Parker grin. At first Mark was puzzled. He studied the face and suddenly realized it could be but one person—Bob Parker. After a few moments' visiting, the two climbed into the shiny car and drove to the brick house in town. Bob didn't know the family had moved into town; so naturally he had gone straight to the ranch. That was home to him.

Our father, Maximillian Parker, at about the age of seventy-six,
taken five years before Bob returned.

Dad, eighty-one, was sitting on the step by the kitchen door of the brick house, enjoying the shade and the late afternoon calm. His hair was white, and he wore a thick white mustache. He was a fine-looking man, straight and alert, and, as always, dressed immaculately. The flashy car drove into the yard, and Mark stepped out. Dad was surprised. That morning Mark had left on horseback, headed for the ranch. Rather slowly the driver slipped out on the left side of the car and straightened up. At first Dad wondered who it was.

Bob's face for once was solemn; perhaps he wondered how he would be accepted. The screen door to the kitchen was open behind Dad's back. Bob took off his hat and twirled it through the door. It landed squarely on the post of the rocking chair inside. Then he grinned that unmistakable grin. Dad knew him. No one could ever describe that meeting after all the years of uncertainty and separation—forty-one years. That reunion proved the strength of Dad's heart; he survived it.

Minutes later my brother Mark appeared at my kitchen door and said, "Lula, we've got company. Dad wants you to come down and fix supper."

That wasn't the first time I had been asked to leave my family and prepare supper for company for Dad and the boys. Pauline was old enough to take care of our children, but John, the baby at that time, set up a howl to go along.

Jose went with me to Dad's. In clean dishtowels I wrapped two loaves of warm bread and a fresh bullberry pie that I had just taken from the oven, and we walked over to Dad's. We walked in the front gate and around to the kitchen door. I glanced at the unfamiliar car and wondered who it was this time. As we stepped into the kitchen, put down the food, and went on into the living room, the conversation stopped. The stranger stood up as I stepped into the room, and I studied his face in the awkward silence. He wasn't a stranger, not really, and yet he was. Why did he look so familiar?

Dad smiled. "I'll bet you don't know who this is." I was puzzled. By his features, he had to be family. "Lula, this is LeRoy!" Dad announced.

My husband, Joseph A. Betenson, 1938.

My jaw dropped. Even though I was sure he was alive and somewhere in the country, I had never anticipated this meeting. Bob grinned. My knees felt like rubber, and my insides turned upside down. Any resentment I had harbored toward my outlaw brother melted. The Prodigal had returned!

We didn't have a fatted calf handy to kill for our feast, but I have never forgotten that meal. I fried lamb chops and fixed mashed potatoes topped with chunks of fresh homemade butter and vegetables right out of the garden and, of course, I had brought the homemade bread. Bob exclaimed, "Lula, your bread is as good as Ma's." His compliments further disarmed me. At last I served dessert. "Bullberry pie! Of all things!" he exclaimed. "Bullberries always have made me homesick. They remind me of Ma." I've always thought that was a coincidence that I should have made bullberry pie on that memorable day.

As our first excitement subsided, Dad said: "At first I thought it was Eb and Mark coming up the walk, but when he grinned, I knew in a minute it was LeRoy."

Bob had never ceased to be a close member of the family, no matter what he had done nor how far away he was. Perhaps, because he was the Prodigal, we were more conscious of him than the others who stayed at home.

That first night, we visited until the wee morning hours. He was surprised at all our nicknames and often wondered whom we were talking about. Intensely interested in talking about Mother, he expressed his deep sorrow for having caused her so much heartache. He knew he had broken her heart. Realization of the sorrow and humiliation he had caused the family had kept him from coming home long before. But he had gone straight for the past sixteen years. Surely that much repentance made him worthy to return. Many times through his outlaw years and after 1909 when he was reported killed in South America, he longed to come home, but his pride wouldn't let him. He was too ashamed.

Dad patted his hand and said, "At last your mother's prayers have been answered. We just couldn't understand why you didn't come."

Bob said he had never forgotten how Mother looked that morning he left in 1884. "I can just see her standing and holding old Dash," he said. Then he repeated the story in great detail, much as I related it in the early part of this book. His account tallied perfectly with Mother's: the blue blanket with food rolled in it, the dog, the poplar trees. How pleased he had been to see them still growing when he arrived at the ranch. He referred to his helping Mother when they brought them from Beaver to plant them.

Repeatedly he steered the conversation back to Mother. He couldn't hear enough of her. He asked about every member of the family—what they were doing, what their children were like. Bob assured us that he and Sundance really intended to go straight when they went to South America, but he said, with a trace of bitterness in his voice, "When a man gets down, they won't let him up. He never quits paying his price." He didn't seem to want to talk about his past or his escapades and did so only as we asked questions.

During the night Bob told us about the friends he had made in South America, about his travels down there and elsewhere. He had a little money, and he wasn't afraid to work. He did a lot of traveling in Europe, especially in Spain, also spending some time in Italy, which he greatly enjoyed. He said the Italians were very warm, friendly people, and he loved them.

He related that he and Sundance did not come back to the United States together after they were supposed to have been killed. As Longabaugh and he were getting ready to leave South America, Bob's leg became badly swollen. He described it as a white swelling. He thought it might have been caused by a scorpion bite. So Sundance went to take care of last-minute business. Bob said, "We were to meet at a certain place, but my leg was so bad I couldn't keep the appointment. An Indian woman took me into her home and doctored me as if I were her own son. She put poultices on the leg until the swelling finally went down. It reminded me of how Ma always took care of wanderers as well as her own children."

Then we told him about the Indian boy whose leg Mother had sagepacked for days, and when we had asked her why she had bothered with him, her reply had been, "If it was LeRoy, I'd want someone to take care of him."

"Yes," Bob agreed thoughtfully, "I remember how she always said, 'Bread cast upon the water will return to you.' " Then he continued. "I spent several weeks at that home, and I never knew what happened to Sundance. When I was strong enough to go on my way, this woman's young son Padro wanted to go with me. I called the little scamp Paddy. We finally persuaded his mother to let him accompany me, with the understanding that I would send him home in a few weeks. I thought if the law was after me, they wouldn't think of apprehending a man with a kid—it would be a perfect blind. And besides, Paddy was good company. We saw parts of South America that I hadn't seen before. Then I outfitted him fit to kill with new clothes, gave him some money, and sent him home. He had a great time with me. Then he had to go back to a quiet home life."

"By gum, you always were taken with the kids. Guess you never got over it," Dad observed.

"Never did," Bob grinned. "But I'll bet Paddy never forgot that trip. And I hope he never forgets what I told him."

"What was that?" Dad asked.

"Told him never to get off the old straight and narrow. Every kid I've ever known I've tried to point in the right direction. My life has been wasted; I don't want to see other kids go wrong. I'd hate to think any boy got off on the wrong track because he thought our life was exciting and thrilling. I've paid the price over and over. Nobody will ever know."

"You could have been a success at anything you wanted, LeRoy," Dad said.

"But there's no such a thing as a successful outlaw. If only I'd come home with you that day you found me in the open cell in Montrose. But no, I was so cockeyed smart—wanted more money before I came home. Well, I've very little to show for my fifty-nine years. 'Easy come, easy go.' I sure didn't hoard my money. I'd like to think I've helped a few people along the way, but I'd better keep my mouth shut. You always told us we shouldn't toot our own horn or blow on ourselves, Dad."

Dad cleared his throat and said, "What did you do after you sent Paddy home?"

"Well, I'd missed my rendezvous with Sundance and had no idea how to get in touch with him. I had nowhere to go, so I drifted on up into Mexico—worked wherever and whenever I wanted to. I wondered what had happened to Sundance—and Etta Place, too. I guess the heat turned off with the shooting when Sundance and I were supposed to have been killed."

"What about that?" Dad asked. "Read a lot in the newspapers and didn't ever know what to believe."

"I read more about it when I came back to the States than I ever knew in South America," Bob said. "Heard it for years."

"It wasn't you then?" Dad prodded.

"I'm here to prove it wasn't." He grinned that unforgettable grin. "And I'm no ghost—no angel either," he winked.

"Just what did happen?" Dad asked.

"I don't really know myself. I heard they got Percy Seibert from the Concordia Tin Mines to identify a couple of bodies as Butch Cassidy and the Sundance Kid all right. I wondered why Mr. Seibert did that. Then it dawned on me that he would know this was the only way we could go straight. I'd been close to Seibert—we'd talked a lot, and he knew how sick of the life I was. He knew I'd be hounded as long as I lived. Well, I'm sure he saw this as a way for me to bury my past along with somebody else's body so I could start over. I'd saved his and Mr. Glass's

184

lives on a couple of occasions, and I guess he figured this was how he could pay me back. Funny thing—Ma always used to say, 'A friend in need is a friend indeed.' "

"I guess you could say some of your mother's bread cast on the water came back to you," Dad said.

"Hadn't thought of it like that, but I suppose you're right," he rubbed his chin thoughtfully.

"Well, by gum, LeRoy, I hope you've learned a lesson." Dad almost bored a hole through him with his sharp eyes.

"I did. Haven't stolen a pin since then and have never done a thing to get the law onto me. I want to stay dead as far as they're concerned. Funny thing though, how many stories I hear about how I escaped."

"We've heard a few ourselves," Dad agreed.

"For example," Bob continued, "one day I was sitting in a hotel lobby in San Francisco, and I overheard these two fellows talking about my demise in South America. Apparently they had read something about it in the newspaper. One fellow went on to tell how 'it really happened.' He knew all the inside dope, he bragged.

"He related that I slipped into the courtyard during that gun battle and pulled a dead soldier inside. Then I removed his uniform, dressed the soldier in my clothes, and donned the uniform. In all the excitement I slipped back outside and got away because no soldier would shoot one of his own men. I was badly wounded. I dragged myself down to the river and got on a raft that was floating by and, half dead, floated down the river—I believe he said it was the Amazon. He might as well make it big while he was telling such a tall tale; the Amazon is only about a thousand miles from Bolivia.

"Well, the raft caught at the side of the river and was found by an Indian woman who was surprised to find one of the soldiers from the gun battle. Don't ask me how she would know of such a thing when communications are so bad down there and most of 'em can't read or write anyhow. Well, this Indian woman, or native woman, called her husband, and they dragged the wounded 'soldier' to their hut and she nursed me back to health and I came back to the United States.

"When people get too inquisitive and ask too many questions, or I feel especially devilish, I've repeated that story a few times myself," he winked.

"By gum, LeRoy, that's a real story—a real tall tale—but if *you* tell it, people will think it's true. You shouldn't do it," Dad objected.

We Parkers always enjoyed a good story, and we laughed about it at the time, never realizing how many times it would be repeated as a true story, straight from "the horse's mouth." Then Dad became very serious. "LeRoy, did you ever kill anyone?"

"No, thank God. But some of my boys had itchy trigger fingers. I tried to control 'em. I feel real bad about some posse men who got shot." He cleared his throat, then changed the subject. "I spent a good bit of time in Mexico. I'm always looking out for the underdog, you know, and the revolution brought on lots of problems, especially with the people in the Mormon colonies in Juarez and Sonora.

"Well, one day I was sitting in a bar in Mexico City, minding my own business, like any law-abiding citizen. I didn't think a soul was looking for me. I was studying the counter absently, with my head down. The bartender put my drink down in front of me. Suddenly I felt a hand grip my shoulder. I didn't dare look up. The hair on the back of my neck stood on end, and that creepy feeling traveled up my scalp. I thought—here it is, after all this time! I realized I had long since ceased to keep up my guard. I gulped real hard and glanced up to see who had apprehended me after all those years. Had Pinkertons finally trapped me? Who should it be but Etta Place standing there! I was so relieved I almost collapsed on the bar stool. She was the same old Etta—a beautiful woman, and she was a helluva good cook. She said she and Sundance had a place in the city, and I went with her. We had a great time visiting together for several days. Then one afternoon we went to a bullfight. I always hated bullfights—couldn't stomach them. After a little while of watching, I picked up my bag and told them three's a crowd. I gave 'em the high sign and left. Our paths have gone in separate directions ever since."

We asked Bob if he really pulled as many jobs as were attributed to him. He laughed, "Horses were too slow to be in Alaska one day and New Mexico the next. I couldn't be in two places at once. The same was true in South America. You know, the cattle-rustling we were blamed for in this country is a joke. I'd like to tell people who the real rustlers were. It sure wasn't the little man but the big shot, with a long rope and a hot iron. I worked for some good, honest men. I think I'm safe in saying I could always go back and get a job."

I asked Butch who was his best friend. He said, "There were a lot of good friends, but Elzy Lay was the best, always dependable and level-headed. Sundance and I got along fine, but he liked his liquor too much and was too quick on the trigger."

He told us how nice Elzy's wife, Maude Davis, was and spoke well of the people in Brown's Park, especially the Bassetts. Josie was his favorite—and the Davises. He told about the Simpson family in Wyoming and Mrs. Simpson in particular. "She reminded me of Ma," he reflected.

His face grew sober as he admitted, "I had every chance to live a good life. Instead I wasted it. We saw some pretty rough times—a lot of fun, too. But you'll never know how I longed to be home at times."

Dad spoke up, "If it hadn't been for that dirty bunch before you left home, you would have been all right. Whatever possessed you to take the blame for the cattle deal?"

"Well, they said they'd pay me well, and I needed the money for my trip. I don't blame 'em altogether. I was old enough to know better. I've only myself to blame."

"Did you ever get anything out of it?"

"Not a dime. All I got was a bad name. I often wondered what drove me to do what I've done in the past. I didn't get any of it at home. We had fun, even if we did have to work hard. When I think of the trouble I've caused you, it really hurts. I don't know how I could've done this to Ma. God knows I loved her. Guess I'm the only black sheep in the family."

This got us all. There was a long silence. Then he broke the spell by saying, "You know, Dad, I never remember ever being licked in my life—and I know I sure needed it, too."

I spoke up, "I guess we can all say that. But when Dad spoke, we listened."

Butch continued. "*You* did. I didn't. So many times I wanted to go straight. I thought going to South America might work, but I couldn't escape my past as long as I lived. Now that I'm supposed to be dead, I really enjoy myself. I'm trying to forget the past. I'll be forever grateful to Seibert for what he did in identifying me.

"I'd been thinking for a long time of coming home and seeing you all and a lot of my old friends. I've visited a lot of cemeteries and have seen a lot of names I thought I'd see. Most of my old cronies have met early, violent deaths. It's no good. Even though I've been lucky enough to survive, let me tell you it's true: crime's no good. I tried to justify my crimes by my bitterness against the big-moneyed thieves, but I was only fooling myself. You have to live with your conscience, and it catches up with you. Even a battered one does."

But no matter what we talked about, he always came back to Mother. He couldn't hear enough of her.

We had heard through the grapevine many stories of Bob's Robin Hood acts of generosity to people who needed a helping hand. I couldn't resist asking him about a couple of those incidents. His face reddened. He nodded as we mentioned them. I had frequently heard about the widow and the mortgage, and he told it with a twinkle in his eye.

"This is a good one—and true. One day I went into a store where I often picked up supplies. It was run by a little widow lady. That day she looked real glum, and I asked her what was the matter. She replied, 'The man who holds the mortgage on this store is coming to collect, and I haven't got the money. He'll take my store.

" 'How much do you owe?' I asked her.

" 'A thousand dollars.' And the tears came to her eyes. 'I just can't make ends meet with my husband dead and gone.'

" 'Now you quit your worrying. Just give me a little time and maybe I can help,' I told her.

" 'But a thousand dollars. That's a fortune.'

"I left the store. When I came back later I gave her ten one hundred dollar bills. Her eyes bugged out. I guess she'd never seen that much before all at once. I warned her, 'Now don't you tell that old skinflint where you got your money. But you make sure you have a signed receipt for it and it's marked paid in full.' Of course, the old lady was really in tears now, but for a different reason. 'Come on now,' I said, 'dry your eyes so that old coot won't suspect anything when he comes.'

"Then I went a little way out of town where I knew he'd be coming along, and I hid in the bushes by the road. Sure enough, in a while his buggy came rattling along. He had the snappiest horses with all the trappings, and he was slicked up fit to kill—black suit and white starched shirt. He was a stuffed shirt all right. I could tell he didn't need that ole lady's store any more than I did. And it made my blood boil to think how he was just waiting to turn her out. He had a self-satisfied smirk on his face. That's what always makes me so damned mad. The rich are too rich and the poor are too poor.

"Well, it wasn't too long before I heard that buggy rattling back down the road. I peeked through the bushes from my hiding place. I wanted to wipe that greedy look off his face the worst way. His buggy slowed down as it got near to my ambush. Now that was mighty convenient. I was surprised when I heard him say 'Whoa!' to his team, and they stopped almost in front of my hiding place.

There wasn't another soul anywhere in sight. He peered around suspiciously, and then he pulled out his billfold and counted to make sure it was all there: 'Nine hundred—one thousand,' he counted out loud.

"I took my cue and stepped out of the bushes, gun in hand. 'I'll take those,' I said. He was so surprised he handed 'em over without an argument, and I slipped out of sight. This was so successful that I paid off more than one mortgage in the same way. In fact, I wasn't the only outlaw who salved his conscience in that way."

I asked Bob about the time he played Santa Claus to a family.

"What story is that?" he asked.

I told him it was when he was almost frozen to death. Often I'd heard that story and wondered if it were true. Here was my chance to verify it. I'm not sure, but I think he said the people's name was Hancock.

He told us this story. "That was the closest I ever got to leaving this earth. I got caught in one of those terrible December blizzards. My clothes were frozen stiff, and I was lost—I mean lost! I'd bought a horse from a fellow the previous May, and he'd told me the horse had homing instincts. So I let the horse have his head. Without my knowing it, the horse headed home for the corral where he'd been raised. I was too cold to worry about anything. It was close to Christmas, and I grew drowsy and dreamy. Suddenly I could hear beautiful music—singing. It was like hearing Ma play the organ and all the kids singing Christmas carols. I was home again and everything was rosy. I wasn't cold any more. I hadn't been that happy since—I couldn't remember when.

"Then I was in agony. The pain in my extremities was excruciating, and it felt like nails were being pounded into my chest when I tried to breathe. First I was burning up, then my teeth were chattering, and I couldn't stop it. Through my fog, I made out a man and woman and a little boy and girl standing around me, rubbing me with snow out of a tub nearby. I groaned in pain. Why didn't they let me go home to stay? I hurt in every inch of my body. Because of the pain in my chest, the man

190

decided I had pneumonia, and he sat up all night putting hot aspen branches over my chest and under my arms. I'd never heard of a cure like that, but it sure worked. They had to cut one of my boots off my frozen foot.

"When I asked him how I'd wound up there, he told me. He'd heard his dogs barking during that terrible storm. When he went outside, he found me almost frozen to death, slumped over a horse at the gate of his corral.

"He got me into the house, and I started to thaw out. When he went back to the corral, he discovered the horse I was riding was really a horse that had been stolen from him the spring before, but he didn't tell me until the next morning.

" 'I'll have you know I bought that horse fair and square. I'll settle the score with that skunk as soon as I can get around,' I told him.

"In a few days I was up and around. I hunted up that skunk who had sold me a stolen horse; he didn't live far away. I demanded a horse in exchange for the stolen one. And then I told him I also wanted a buckboard and a team to use for a few days.

"I'd learned the Hancocks were real poor nesters. They'd been cheated by land speculators and were living in a two-room shack. But they'd shared with me the little they had. I knew there wouldn't be much Christmas at their house that year, so I went into town in the buckboard and bought warm clothes for the family. I bought a sweater for the lady to wear around the house because it was so cold and drafty. And I got plenty of food. Then I picked up all the other makings of a Christmas and headed back to the Hancocks'. Those little kids had been so cute. They'd climbed all over me and about worn out my ears with their Christmas chatter. It had been like being home when the house was full of our little ones.

"Well, when I reached that shack again, I was so busy unloading all that loot and was so excited myself with the fun of being Santa Claus, that I hadn't noticed three horsemen ride up. Suddenly I looked up and saw a sheriff's badge on the coat of one of the riders. My heart sank, but I went right on unloading, figuring this was the end of the road for me. Well, at least I was having a good time, and I was doing something worthwhile for a change. I couldn't help thinking how much better it would have been if the Hancocks had let me freeze to death rather than go to prison again. But then they'd never have had a Christmas if I had died.

"The Hancocks stood there as puzzled as anything; then Mrs. Hancock hurried and hid the kids' presents.

"When I finished unloading, I straightened up and said, 'Well, I guess this is it. Suppose I should thank you, Hancock, for saving my life, but I don't rightly know what for. Maybe it was to spread a little Christmas cheer—the real Christmas cheer.'

"The sheriff scratched his head and said knowingly, 'I've got a warrant here for George LeRoy Parker. Seen him around?'

" 'Sure,' I grinned. 'He was camping not far from here just a few days ago.'

" 'If you see him around, tell 'im I'm lookin' fer 'im.' The sheriff tipped his hat, smiled and winked, and rode off. 'Merry Christmas. Come on, boys, we'd better be on our way.' And that's as close as I ever got to being thrown in jail again."

All night long we talked. He told of leaping into the river when they were being trailed, but I doubt it was as dramatic as in the movie. He told of his efforts to go straight and how frustrated he was when the railroad was going to employ him, but the meeting at the Pass was never consummated.

Bob told us that after leaving Mexico, he went to Alaska, where he trapped and prospected. He lived with the Eskimos for a short time and told how they were being cheated and fleeced by dishonest speculators. He hated to see innocent people duped. But Alaska was too cold for him, and he stayed there only a year or two. He liked the Northwest, and that was home to him.

"Why don't you come home where you belong, LeRoy?" Dad asked. "There's nothing against you on the books in Utah." (Jose, my husband, had gone to Salt Lake City sometime before this and had checked it out.)

Bob shook his head. "No, I don't belong here any more, Dad. I've got other things to see about. And I want to travel around and see my old friends. Just keep this under your hat—my visit here, I mean."

Dad nodded thoughtfully. "If that's what you want, that's the way it will be." He turned to the rest of us and said, "This is our secret. You are never to mention it to anyone. If you want a secret kept, never tell it." And we never did. Even other members of our own family didn't know it for years. I think Butch was going under the name of Bob Parks at the time.

No one wondered about the strange car at the brick house in Circleville; company was not unusual there. I remember that Jim Martin (the Parker boys nicknamed him Linky Jim) had come and stayed one whole winter. Company came and went. Circleville is laid out like most early Mormon towns, with four houses to a block, one on each corner; so there were no close neighbors.

We knew Bob was no angel, and in our conversations he didn't try to paint himself as one, either. He told us about South America and only a little about their life there and about Etta Place. He stayed with Dad a couple of days; then he and Mark went up to the hills in Dog Valley, southwest of Circleville, to visit with his brothers, who had a cabin up there.

Bob and Mark rode out to the camp on horseback. At first my brothers couldn't make out who it was. Then as the riders rode closer, and Bob's face broke into that disarming grin, they knew who it was.

My son, Mark Betenson (eleven years old then), working with my brothers at their camp, was out gathering wood when the "stranger" arrived. When Mark came into the cabin with an armload, Eb said, "This is Lula's son." But nobody told Mark who the stranger was. They ate supper, guarding their conversation, then scooted Mark off for home so they could talk freely.

When young Mark came home, he said, "There's this man at the cabin. I think they said he was from Colorado. Anyway, they called him Bob. There wasn't room enough for me, so they sent me home." He was quite put out, to say the least.

Many years later Mark was talking with Eb about that day the strange man came to the cabin, and Eb told him who it was. Mark kept the secret faithfully until one day when he and I were chatting, and he asked me very confidentially if I knew that "Uncle Butch" had come home a long time ago. When he was sure I, too, shared the secret, we discussed it often.

My other children never knew about this until the last several years. John distinctly remembers how he howled to go with me that night, and I made him stay with Pauline. Barbara must have been eighteen when Jose accidentally mentioned something about Butch Cassidy being her uncle. This was the first she had ever heard of it, and I was miffed at Jose for mentioning it. This proves how little was said to any of us by the townspeople and how close-mouthed we all were about our "secret."

Bob spent about a week with the boys and a day or two more with Dad in town. Then he left and never returned. Occasionally Dad had a letter from him, but his letters were always carefully destroyed to protect Bob. We worried about what trouble it might cause him if they fell into the wrong hands. Who would ever have dreamed that a letter from Butch Cassidy would be valuable! He must have kept up a lively correspondence with his friends; I have learned of many who reported letters coming to their home from Butch Cassidy. Most of the letters were destroyed for the same reason that we destroyed them. Some were saved but have since been stolen or lost, and to date I have never been able to find one.

One day Dad received a letter from one of Bob's friends, reporting that Bob had died of pneumonia. The letter assured Dad that his son was "laid away very nicely." It was signed simply "Jeff."

Robert LeRoy Parker died in the Northwest in the fall of 1937, a year before Dad died. He was not the man who was known as William Phillips, reported to be Butch Cassidy.

Although we have received a couple of reports to the contrary, so far as we know Butch was never married. I am sure that if he had been, he would have told us; and if he'd had any children, you can be sure he would have taken care of them, and we would have known. Where he is buried and under what name is still our secret. Dad said, "All his life he was chased. Now he has a chance to rest in peace, and that's the way it must be." Revealing his burial place would furnish clues for the curious to crack that secret. *I* wouldn't be a Parker if I broke my word.

To further emphasize my concern for keeping his burial place a secret, may I relate a significant incident. My son Mark, who runs the old Parker Ranch near Circleville, had a man doing some leveling on a part of the property. Some time previously Mark had buried his old dog Hummerdo, to which his family was greatly attached. All our lives, we've buried animals because of sentiment. So, on that particular day, Mark said to the workman, "Just stay away from the corner over there on the hill. There's a grave there, and I don't want it disturbed." Next day, Circleville was buzzing with the rumor that Butch Cassidy was buried at the ranch.

Another well-meaning person who claims to know where the Banditti Americanos were supposed to have been buried after the battle of San Vicente wanted to contact Bolivian authorities and have their bodies exhumed and sent to me at Circleville for burial on the Parker Ranch. I have since heard that the two have been exhumed, and that saddens me. Of course, the exhumation was for identification purposes, and it proved that the two who were buried were not bandits, as had been believed.

Still other incidents disturb me by their implications. Sam Brannon, prominent in early Mormon history and in settling an area in northern California, died as a pauper in Escondido, California. Many months after

Brannon's death, a nephew of his was located who claimed the body from the morgue and had Brannon buried in the Mt. Hope Cemetery in San Diego. The grave was marked by a redwood slab that deteriorated with time and weather. A kindly woman was instrumental in soliciting funds so that a simple permanent marker might be installed. However, in the last several years a few people have been agitating to have his remains moved to northern California where he would be suitably honored.

In the newspaper I have recently read that Johnny Herring's body was dug up, and I was hurt to see the gruesome pictures. This exhumation has also happened to other outlaws recently.

Who knows what might spring into the minds of either some hero-worshippers or some debunkers in another fifty years? It is entirely possible that some person or persons would want to make a memorial out of my brother's burial spot if it were known. This would amount to glorifying his misspent life, an honor certainly not according to his wishes nor the wishes of the family.

If I were to reveal his burial place, someone would be sure to disturb it under some pretext, and my brother is entitled to rest in peace.

The Legend Lives On
Chapter 16

       I have been amazed at the many people who have written me and volunteered information on Butch and the Wild Bunch. My heartfelt thanks go out to them. I am accepting the reports as they come to me with no effort to verify them. Some letters offer substantiation of many of my own claims about the personality and conduct of my brother. Therefore, I should like to include excerpts from a few of these letters and interviews and also to quote articles by, or about, individuals who knew of his return to the United States from South America.*

       Cowboy Joe (Joseph Claude Marsters) saw Butch in 1915 after he was supposed to have been killed in South America. A newspaper article is quoted here:

       Cowboy Joe said the last time he saw Butch Cassidy was at the Wild West Show in San Francisco (Joe Miller's) in 1915. Joe had just made a spectacular ride on a bucking steer while shooting his six-shooter loaded with blank cartridges into the air. A "dressed up cowhand" jumped over the fence and into the arena and complimented him on his ride. "He said my old boss thought I

---

*Editor's note: Original spelling, grammar, and sentence structure have been retained in these letters to preserve their flavor and authenticity.

John Hardy of Milford, Utah, says this is a picture of Butch taken in Juarez, Mexico. *Courtesy of John Hardy.*

had improved my riding since he had last seen me. Looking up in the direction the cowboy was pointing, up in the audience, all leaving now that the show was over, Butch, with that big bright smile he often displayed, threw up his arm, so as I could locate him. He didn't appear to want to carry the incident farther." [1]

John Hardy of Milford, Utah, gave me a picture of Butch which had been given to him by his mother-in-law, Mrs. H. E. Bowman. The Bowmans lived in the Mormon colonies in Juarez, Mexico, and were driven out in 1912 by the revolutionists.

Mrs. Bowman told Mr. Hardy that this picture was taken in Juarez during the Mexican Revolution. She said the Mexican soldiers had captured her husband and were going to kill him, but at that strategic moment Butch appeared and informed the captors he would tell them where to find Pancho Villa if they would let Mr. Bowman go. Although the soldiers doubted him, they released their captive.

The Bowmans moved to Texas, where Mr. Bowman worked in the customs house in El Paso. One day Butch rode into the Bowman farm at Paradale, Texas, on a beautiful horse. He stayed at the Bowman farm long enough to grow a full beard before going back into Old Mexico. Again here was a brief home-away-from-home. Everyone on the place had a great liking for Tod McClamy (the alias by which Butch was known there).

One night Tod McClamy heard the Bowmans' six-year-old daughter saying her prayers. She asked the Lord to "bless Tod McClamy." Butch turned to Mrs. Bowman and said, "That's enough to make anybody go straight."

The Bowmans moved to Kanab, Utah, in 1915. Their association with Butch was limited to the years 1910 to 1915, long after he was supposed to have been killed in

1. Kerry Ross Boren, "Butch and The Kid: Did They Return from South America?" *Salt Lake Tribune*, 11 June 1972.

South America. The above information was related in a letter to me from Mr. Hardy dated September 29, 1972, as his recollections of the many times Mrs. Bowman had related these incidents to him before she died.

I quote here from other letters I have received:

Cle Elum, Washington
June 15, 1974

Mrs. Lula Parker Betenson

Dear Mrs. Betenson:
In late October, 1914, a friend Albert Wright walked up to a man on the street in Ogden, Utah and put out his hand and said Hello Butch, and turned to me and said, Slim meet my friend Butch Cassidy. And in 80 years I have not had a more friendly hand shake.

Sincerely,
J. E. Howard

Dec. 5, 1970

Dear Mrs. Lula Betenson:
I am writing this letter to you to tell you of the fond friendship that was between my father H. E. Hank Boedeker and your brother Butch Cassidy. And it lasted intill Butch came back to Dubois and Lander in 1929. They roomed togeather in the old Cottage Home Hotel in Lander in the late 80's when my father was hauling lumber off the mountain south of Lander for Charley Buntes. . . .
In 1929 when I was running the old Frontier Cafe in Dubois Wyo. Butch Cassidy and two young fellows came in the cafe and had T-bones. And Butch talked to me for hours asking me all about the old timers around Lander like Mell Baldwin, Orson Grimmet and Ed Lanigan who run the Lanigan saloon.
Later he ask me if Hank Boedeker was still alive and I told him yes he was still marshall in Lander at that

time. Butch Cassidy had come back to Wyo to try to find a cash they had buryed up on the old Washaki trail. . . .

Butch told about the shoot-out in South America and how bad the Sundance Kid got shot up and how he traded clothes with a dead man and took the swag and lived in the timber. . . . He hit a big river and went down it to the mouth and it was the Amazon and there was a tramp steamer tied up there and he got back to the states. . . . I all so remember one time Butch was hid out on Weggins Fork my Father packed him in some grub. He was known as the Robinhood of the west. . . .

Most of my brothers met him in 1929.

Truly yours,
W. H. Boedeker

This letter bears out the fact that Butch repeated his wild story about the gun battle when he felt especially devilish, and it was accepted as fact. No wonder there are so many legends.

Lander, Wyoming, Apr. 1, 1968

Dear Mrs. Betenson:

Yesterday, March 31st was Dora Lamoreaux Robertson's 94th birthday. Her daughter, Irene, staged a big reception and birthday party. Dora was the youngest acting person there. There were over a hundred at the party which was held at the Pioneer Museum.

I told the gathering about the professor from Brigham Young U that came over to see me and get him in touch with someone who knew Butch. I took him to Carl Obert, now dead, to Mrs. Henry Farlow, also dead and to Dora. I told him that Dora had kept company with Butch. He asked me, "Do you suppose they ever necked?" I told the prof I didn't know but he would have to ask her; I wouldn't. I took him out to the ranch and it was something to see. He said to Dora, "I have been informed that you kept company with Butch Cassidy." Dora said, "Yes, I

201

did." Then he asked, "What did you and Butch do when you were together?" Dora said, "We went horseback riding, out to the oil wells and Ft. Washakie." "Well, what else did you do?" It finally dawned on Dora what he was after and she told him in no uncertain tones, "I'll have you know when Butch Cassidy was with me, he was a perfect gentleman and I was a lady." That sure shut him up. I told the story before the crowd yesterday. Dora don't look like she was 94; she could pass for a woman of fifty. . . .

Dora is the only one alive that knew Butch, by the way. I saw some pictures of him. It shows a cabin, said it was at Robbers Roost 2. I believe the picture was the old Quien Sabe Ranch. It was a hold-out of the Wild Bunch. The picture lists as George Parker. I don't know how the George got tangled up. I know he was christened Robert LeRoy Parker.

Old Tom Osborn, owner of the Quien Sabe Ranch, was in Casper one day in 1893 stocking up on provisions and picked up a man named Thorn who was down on his luck. Thorn was hungry. Old Tom took him to a restaurant for breakfast and took him back to the ranch and gave him a job. Thorn learned that old Tom couldn't read or write. He asked old Tom to let him work out the price of a saddle horse. Old Tom agreed. He then asked old Tom to give him a bill of sale. Instead of a bill of sale it was a deed to the ranch and all the livestock.

A few days after Thorn had filed the deed in the County Clerk's office in Lander, Old Tom was riding the range and ran across a neighbor, Liams. Liams said, "I see you've sold the ranch and all the livestock." Old Tom said, "Hell, I aint sold any ranch or live stock." Liams said, "Well, Thorn filed a deed in the County Clerk's office in Lander." It dawned on Old Tom that he had been crooked and how. He said, "I'll kill that s.o.b. if it's the last thing I do." Thorn, in the meantime, had some misgivings. He went across the street to Jim Patten's drug store and told Old Jim, "Jim, that old Tom Osborn has been threatening to kill me. Do you suppose he'll try?"

Old Jim said, "Old Tom Osborn wouldn't hurt a fly." That same afternoon Old Tom came riding into

Lander, ties his horse to the hitching rack in front of the old Lanagan saloon. As he opened the front door, Thorn made for the back with Old Tom hot after him. Old Tom got one shot at him. Thorn staggered into a Chinese restaurant and collapsed. They arrested Old Tom and Judge Jesse Knight sentenced him to 7 years in the pen. The deed to the ranch was cancelled and Old Tom deeded the ranch to Butch Cassidy. Butch held the ranch until Old Tom was pardoned out by Governor Richards and Butch deeded the ranch back to him.

Yours truly,
Bill Marion

In an interview for the *Casper Star Tribune*, Wednesday, October 16, 1968, Mr. Marion explained a bit more about Butch's ownership of the Quien Sabe Ranch on Hoodoo Creek:

Two years ago I took a metal detector to the Old Quien Sabe Ranch. I got no reaction around the old ranch house. My son-in-law, Dr. L. E. McGonigle, took the detector down on Hoodoo Creek about a mile from the ranch house. He got a reaction. We dug up where the detector howled and the needle climbed high. In a couple of feet we dug up some mason jars, some three or four that would hold a half gallon. All were broken. The metal covers gave the detector the reading. I am positive that was where Old Butch had a cache.

Charl Hanks, who lives at Green River, Utah, remembers my brother well. He verifies Butch's death as a result of pneumonia:

Butch was a helluva fine fellow. Always friendly and cheerful and one of the best horsemen I ever knew. And he was not killed in South America as the Pinkertons say. I had a letter for a long time that proved he died in Oregon of pneumonia at the age of 73, I loaned the letter to Charles Hunt, who was writing a history of this country, and now he can't find it. Also Will Pace of Duchesne saw Butch right here in Green River after he came back from South America, and he knew Butch as well as I know you.[2]

A letter to me from Mrs. Jess Chamberlin, Arapahoe, Wyoming, dated May 24, 1972, tells of an association with Butch in 1933:

I myself did not know your brother Butch Cassidy. But my husband and my father-in-law knew him and camped in the mountains on or about the year 1933 with him. Butch came supposedly on a fishing trip. But most of the Bunch that he visited said he had come to look for his cache which they said he found. When he rode into camp after being out all day they asked him what luck did you have? And he said—Alright. He came out here to see his old friend Will Boyd. . . . I didn't get to see him. . . .

A cousin of Butch's and mine sent me this letter:

Aug. 29, 1972

Dear Lula:
. . . In 1923 I was with the government. We were blasting in the bottom of the canyon where the Boulder Dam now is. A very powerful boat with three men in it came chugging upstream. They said they were prospectors. They wanted food, gasoline and oil. I had charge of all of the supplies. So it was left to me to get what they wanted. I knew one of them was Butch by the questions he asked me. He was familiar with the terrain and many of the people in southern Utah. He asked how "Uncle Brig and Aunt Ada" was. [Cliff's parents and aunt and uncle to Butch and me.] A few days after they were gone, a friend asked me what relation one of them was to me. He said

2. Pearl Baker, "He Rode with Butch," *Salt Lake Tribune*, 8 November 1959.

one of them looked enough like me to be my brother. I have been told before I looked like him. . . .

> *As ever (signed) Cliff*
> *Clearfield, Utah*

And this letter came from the daughter of someone who had known Butch:

> *Lander, Wyo. Sept. 6, 1972*

Dear Mrs. Betenson:
. . . In 1936 I worked in M. N. Baldwin Co's ready-to-wear—in fact, I worked in the store for 20 years. One of the owners came over to me and said Butch Cassidy is over here in the grocery store, that joined the dept. store, so I meandered over to see him. I was a little shy. I'm so sorry I didn't talk to him and tell him who I was. He was a short man (pretty plump) dark suit and good looking hat. Wish I had called my mother to come and see him, because she had known Butch when he was in Lander in his younger days. . . .

> *Irene Lane, daughter of Dora Robertson*

The following letter was written to Dorothy Hubbard, the granddaughter of John and Margaret Simpson:

> *Zortman, Mont.*
> *Jan. 9 /71*

Dear Mrs. Hubbard
Rec'd your letter yesterday and thot now was a good time to answer it, as its snowing out and turning cold. The article you saw in the paper was partly true. To begin with we came over from the snowy Mts in 1898. I was around 6 yrs old at the time. We were put in a boarding school at St. Pauls Mission and that's where I got to know the Curry

Kid Currie's gun. *Courtesy of E. Dixon Larson.*

boys along with Butch Cassidy. That wasn't his right name, I never got to talk to him but new him by sight. They were often down to the Mission as the Curry boys had an uncle Old John Graham. He was a cobbler for the school. The boys would come once a month to see how he was making out, as he was 90 years old at the time and crippled with rhmetism. It was my job to take his meals to him when he was ailing sometimes he couldn't walk. The boys would bring him whiskey enough to keep him going. He died in 1908.

That's how I came to be acuainted with the boys. Loney had a saloon at Harlem. I never new him. In 1918 my father-in-law and my family decided to go near the mountains at the old Butch Cassidy place for a picnic as it was the 4th of July. We were making lunch when this modle A drove up with 2 old men in it. I knew Butch the minute I saw but I didn't greet him and lucky I didn't. My father-in-law knew him well also as he used to work with the Currys. He called him Shorty and that was good enough for me. I asked my father-in-law if that wasn't Butch Casidy he said yes but be careful what you call him. That's Shorty Parker. That's all I can tell you about him, he was supposed to get killed in South America but I know he wasn't.

> As ever
> Chas Kelsey

On page 135 of his book, *Where the Old West Stayed Young*, John Rolfe Burroughs reveals information about some appearances of Butch after his alleged death:

> When I questioned him, Tom Vernon, venerable unofficial "Mayor" of the unincorporated town of Baggs, Wyoming, smiled and nodded in the direction of the two-story frame building which still carries a sign reading: The Vernon Hotel. "Killed in South America—hell!" he exclaimed. "Butch Cassidy came by—I forget the exact year but it was sometime in the twenties—and stayed with me for two days. There's no mistake. I played at the dances he and the other members of the Wild Bunch threw in

Baggs . . ." and Vernon pointed to the old log building in which the Wild Bunch threw their parties.

And, sitting in a rocking chair on the veranda of his home in Green River City, Wyoming, Tom Welch, a huge man, who even at the age of ninety-one conveys an impression of vitality and rugged strength, said: "If Butch Cassidy was killed in South America like they say he was, I had a couple of drinks of whisky in a Lander, Wyoming, bar fifteen years later with a mighty lively ghost!"

Similarly, John Taylor, retired Rock Springs garage man and auto dealer, told me: "One day in 1922 Butch Cassidy drove into the shop in a Model T to get some work done on the car. He was pulling a two-wheel trailer loaded with camping gear. He asked me a lot of questions about old-timers around Rock Springs. He didn't tell me who he was, but I recognized him. . . ."

Lastly, Butch Cassidy's one-time Brown's Park flame, Josephine Bassett Morris, at the age of eighty-six living by herself in a little log cabin with a dirt floor on a ranch 15 miles up the Green River from Jensen, Utah, which she homesteaded in 1919, said: "I saw Butch Cassidy when he came back from South America. I was living in Rock Springs at the time. I had been keeping a hotel in Baggs until my boys were old enough to go to high school, then I moved to Rock Springs. Cassidy and Elzy Lay had come to Rock Springs. They were in a saloon, and Bert Kraft, the bartender, told them about me being in town.

"Butch spoke up and said: 'I'd kind of like to see Josie again,' so Bert Kraft called me on the phone, and made a date. That evening Butch and Elzy came to the house and we had a good visit, talking over old times. Both of them were out of condition, and carried too much weight. . . ."

For a long moment Josie sat silent, staring straight ahead, her mind turned inward. Then: "Butch Cassidy died in Johnny, Nevada," she volunteered. "Don't know the date, but he was an old man."

Reid Burnham of Bountiful, Utah, was raised in Price, Utah, also a mecca for early-day outlaws. Reid's

208

father, Wilbur Burnham, and his mother lived on a ranch north of Price, and Matt Warner was a close neighbor. They had been friends from the 1890s. When the Warners and Burnhams moved into town, this friendship continued. Reid remembers that his father and Matt spent many hours playing cards and drinking in the old Utah Bar. At his mother's impatient request, Reid would have to go down to the bar to tell his father to come home. Only eight or ten at the time, he didn't enjoy these experiences.

As a very young man, Wilbur Burnham worked in the Milburn Saloon in Price with Chub Milburn. In fact, the two ran the saloon for quite a long time when Chub's father went to Alaska hunting for gold.

When Wilbur was about sixteen, he decided he would join the outlaws as their cook. It sounded exciting. His first trip out with them was in May, 1898, the year after the Castle Gate robbery. Young Wilbur was putting the frying pan on the coals just as a posse rode up and opened fire on the unsuspecting group, who had not been involved in the robbery at all. Two of those outlaws were killed (Johnny Herring one of them), and Wilbur didn't have to be coaxed to give up that life. It was his first and last experience. He was glad to go back to work in the saloon.

One day in the saloon, Wilbur was talking to Chub, and Butch Cassidy became the subject of the conversation. Wilbur said, "I've never seen Butch Cassidy."

Chub said, "The heck you haven't. Who do you think you were serving this afternoon? That was Butch Cassidy." Wilbur knew he had served that same man several times before but hadn't known who he was.

Reid said:

Many years later, Dad and I were talking one day and I don't recall just what brought Butch Cassidy

into our conversation, but I remember making the statement, "It's sure too bad he was killed in South America."
Dad said, "Don't you believe it. He didn't die in South
America. He came here to see Matt Warner before and
after his [Matt's] death." But I couldn't get him to say
much more about Butch Cassidy. That always impressed
me, because he told me a lot of stories about other outlaws
and about Robbers' Roost. But he was careful not to talk
about Butch Cassidy. I can see why now. He knew he was
still alive and he wouldn't say a word that might betray
him in any way. My impression from Dad was that Butch
would have come to Price in the early 1930s but I make no
pretense in establishing an exact time. I simply don't
know, but I do know that Dad knew he was alive.

Esther Campbell, wife of Duward Campbell in
Brown's Park, has written me concerning Duward's recollections of Butch Cassidy when he was a boy.

May, 1974

As nearly as he remembered about it, he was
about 11 or 12 years old, living with his father, Ernest
Cheatam Campbell. He spent his winters with his father
going to school in Ft. Worth, Texas and his summers in
Utah and Colorado with his mother. During the summers
he worked for Willis L. Johnson, a cattle man in the area;
and that way Duward learned all about the surrounding
country. Duward's mother and father were separated, and
about that time, Mr. Campbell was paying attention to a
Mrs. June Moore, whom he later married. Mrs. Moore's
husband, at that time was head man of the Moore Com-
mission House in Ft. Worth.
On these visits when Mr. Campbell went to see
June, he always took Duward and a man by the
name of E. S. Cassidy with him. Duward and Cassidy
obtained a room at a small hotel where they stayed
until Campbell came back.
During their time together Duward and Cassidy
visited and ate bananas (which were cheap there then).

210

Cassidy asked questions and they talked about different people he had known around Vernal and Jensen, also about certain locations, such as the Ice Caves and other spots in the Brush Creek area north of Vernal.

Cassidy never told Duward his real name and he was too young to realize what was what. But in later years he pieced together all he had learned and remembers and knew that the man who had been his friend was Butch Cassidy.

Campbell was the Superintendent of the branch office (out of Scranton, Penn.) of the International Correspondence School in Ft. Worth, I think. He gave E. S. Cassidy employment as a traveling salesman for the school over a certain area in Texas.

Duward remembers his father telling Cassidy, "We'll go out and buy you some new clothes, that will be more suitable for your job." They bought some new style "city" clothes and dressed him up as a distinguished-looking city-bred salesman. This must have been about 1913 or 14.

Duward told me this story three or four times. The details were always the same . . . I may be able to find a little more on it, that I may have forgotten, when I get time to look through my papers in "the drawer." He told us this now about two weeks before he died, when he was hardly able to talk.

After their separation, Duward's mother used to write to Mr. Campbell, unbeknowns to June, for money. They used E. S. Cassidy as their go-between—both directions.

Upon inquiry at the International Correspondence School, we learned that their employment files do not date back that far.

The following letter reveals a child's admiration of Butch:

Oct. 15, 1973

Dear Mrs. Betenson:
I hear you are finally going to tell the truth that Butch was not killed in South America. You may well

211

think this was a family kept secret. It was about 4 states kept secret—many knew he was back.

I first met Butch in Dubois, Wyoming when I was 4 years old (1921). He saved my life and my little brother's life. I was an expert swimmer but we kids were disobeying Mom, Dad and Mr. Lemon (my good friend Calvin Lemon who was also a good friend of Butch). We were up at the big ditch which is above the Lemon property. The beaver had built a dam. My little brother couldn't swim and he'd gotten in over his head and got caught in the dam. There were about 6 kids there and I went in to get my brother but couldn't get him loose. The yelling of the other kids brought Butch, who was staying with Mr. Lemon, racing up the hill. Mr. Lemon followed but he was a cripple and couldn't move fast.

Butch hit that water fully dressed and nearly drowned me. He tore my brother loose and pumped the water out of him. Then he whipped every kid there including me. Then we got it again when Dad came home. . . .

My Dad was a U. S. Marshall before I was born but he wasn't the only law man that knew Butch was about. Everyone around Lander, Riverton, Dubois and Baggs, in Utah, [and] Colorado knew he was there. It was no hoax. It was just people minding their own business. Besides Butch had helped too many small ranchers for anyone to give him away. . . .

To me he was a kind, gentle friend and he loved me as a child. He told me great stories. . . . When I first met him his hair was still sandy and he was still good looking. I think it was the greatest hoax ever pulled on the Pinkertons and all the people involved kept their mouth shut—they did this because the law had been rough on the Indians, small ranchers and poor people. There wasn't an Indian who would give him away. I don't know of anyone who had more friends or respect. . . . I saw Butch in April of 1934. Cal Lemon was very ill and dying. Butch came to see him. He stayed with me. . . .

(signed) Laura Hall

The following letter evidences the hero-worship of my brother by some of the members of this generation:

Even though I am in the army and halfway around the world from my friends and family, my interest in the old west is still active. It was with a great deal of surprise that I received a newspaper article about you from a friend back home in Pennsylvania.

It seems almost impossible to me that Butch Cassidy's sister is still in good health there in Utah and it is my wish that the Lord continues to be good to you as He has been in the past.

Did you actually see Butch after that now-famous fight in Bolivia? If he is buried in America will you permit me to send you some money to purchase flowers for his grave as my way of showing the feeling that I have toward him and his career?

[Name withheld]
Stationed in Korea

Two nice young men, whose names I shall withhold, biked all the way from Jacksonville, Florida, to visit me because they are Butch fans and were eager to meet his sister.

Jim Kiick and Larry Csonka, professional football players for the Dolphins in Florida, caught the intrigue of Butch Cassidy and the Sundance Kid from the movie and for kicks (no pun intended) took to dressing up in outfits of the period and riding their horses down the boulevards. Some outlaw signals were even heard in the huddle. Al Levine called me long distance and afterwards wrote an article for the *Miami News* about them. On November 5, 1972, a TV short was shown during the half-time of their game, showing the two dressed-up players riding their horses into the sunset.

I am greatly surprised at the number of columnists and article writers who have visited me and have interviewed me across the country by telephone. Interest in Butch seems to grow instead of to diminish.

A Salt Lake City columnist, Dan Valentine, spent considerable time in London and found that people there are also curious about Butch Cassidy. They plied him with questions. Unfortunately they have the mistaken idea that we still live in log cabins in the West and that the famous outlaws are alive and robbing banks and taking off for the hills on horseback. They don't realize that the western United States has, along with the rest of the world, graduated to highjacking.

From Ireland I have received many letters from a man who knew one of Butch's closest friends in South America. He said, "You know and I know that Butch Cassidy didn't die in South America."

Of all the people I have talked to and heard from, not one has a bad word for my brother. Without exception they all liked him and respected him. Josie Bassett Morris has been quoted as saying, "Butch took care of more poor people than FDR, and with no red tape."

A number of people have told me he paid their taxes when they didn't have the means. Bob's generosity was a reflection of his home training. When he had the money, he gave it where he thought it would do the most good.

The old Parker Ranch, three miles south of Circleville, where Bob lived as a boy, has been designated as a Utah Historical site. The farming operations at the ranch have been carried on for many years by my son Mark. Many nephews were to be considered in the inheritance of the ranch. It seemed wrong to break it up to be equally divided among all heirs; no one would have enough to make it worthwhile. So Eb and Joe Rawlins, my brothers who owned it, decided to settle the inheritance question by having each nephew draw for the highest card. My son Mark won with the king of clubs.

Through the years as Mark drove from town to work on the ranch, he became increasingly shocked at having saddles and branding irons stolen, along with anything else that could be carried off. Even the fireplace was undermined by souvenir seekers who walked off with bricks. Floor planks and even nails were carted away. At

(Top). The old corral at Parker Ranch, still in use today. *Courtesy of Parker Hamilton, Flagstaff, Arizona.*

(Bottom). The old home at Parker Ranch in Circle Valley. *Courtesy of Gladys Hesser Burnham, Bountiful, Utah.*

last, reluctantly, Mark decided to open the ranch to the public, and this remedied the pilfering for a time. Travelers could relax in the shade of the old poplar trees. There were relics of bygone days to see, and the children loved to perch on the fence and watch ranch activities. The flood of people coming from all over the world, but mostly from the United States, was very surprising.

Then in June, 1973, we were shocked and deeply hurt that the ranch was broken into one night. The locks were picked, and a complete housecleaning took place. Irreplaceable items were taken, such as my grandfather's watch and his cane with the letters "RP" carved in it. A history had also been carved on it through various kinds of leaves up and down the cane. It was valued at hundreds of dollars. Grandmother Gillies's original and very large portrait in a beautiful wide gold frame was taken, along with my mother's large portrait in an oval frame, my brother Joe Rawlins's military picture, and many other pictures and furnishings that can't be replaced. This took the heart out of Mark, and the ranch is now closed to the public, although tourists frequently pull off the road to look.

I sincerely hope that those who stop there will be reminded of an unusual man with a mixture of the good and bad that is in all of us. Ed Kirby claims that in Butch's life we see none of the social or personal conflicts that produce bitter men, such as Jesse James, the Younger brothers, or Billy the Kid. I disagree to an extent with his conclusion; my brother did have cause for disillusionment on more than one occasion—beginning with the bishop's court who ruled in favor of the claim jumpers of our parents' land and continuing with unscrupulous mortgage holders and big investors who trampled the rights of the "little guy" under their feet. Butch got into serious trouble backlashing "legal dishonesty" in high places and the in-

216

My son Mark and I at the old Parker Ranch home. The wagon wheels, no longer there, were stolen in 1974. *Courtesy of Gladys Hesser Burnham, Bountiful, Utah.*

justices committed by supposedly reputable men in the name of big business.

The truth is, though, Butch was not a bitter man. I honestly believe he became a victim of his early choices, which led him into deeper trouble. And I believe, with Ed Kirby, that he valued his freedom above everything. He was a man of the land, a liberty-loving, back-country man.

I, too, have no doubt that he could have become anything he chose. Perhaps, as a congressman or a senator, he could have championed the underdog. But before he could mature intellectually, he had plunged into a life of crime.

What I do not believe is that he committed all the crimes credited to him; he could not have survived that long. However, as long as he lived, he was trapped by his reputation; he could not escape it. Only after he was declared dead could he change his ways, and he did.

Strangely, the years have seemed to remove the stigma of his waywardness. In a way this disturbs me, for then he becomes a hero, and he would not have had it that way. One of the concerns that he expressed to us on his return was that daring kids tried to copy the Bunch's methods. He always tried to steer youths away from the bad life back to a home influence. But he couldn't escape the knowledge that his reputation had contributed to their restlessness. His unfortunate choices affected not only his life and the lives of many hero-worshiping young people but also the lives of his entire family who dearly loved him, in spite of, and not because of, what he did. He literally broke my mother's heart. He knew that, and the knowledge grieved him to the end of his life.

Even though the world paints him as one who "got away" with his wrongdoing, don't you believe it. Butch Cassidy, my brother, paid a high price.

My son Mark Betenson, who now owns the Ranch, dressed to imitate Butch for the Circleville Centennial.

More About Butch

In this book Butch's sister, Lula, has asked and has attempted to answer questions about her brother, including searching for reasons for his generosity and for the respect and loyalty he commanded in those who knew him.

We believe some of these reasons are to be found in the following pages—Lula's reminiscences about her childhood and family—charming and nostalgic episodes that reveal a wholesome way of life.

If knowing more about a person's background—the milieu from which he came—can answer some of the questions about his personality and character, these memories from out of his sister's past should solve a part of the riddle that was Butch Cassidy's charisma.

—The Editors

Standing before our old brick home in Circleville brings me
memories of family and home.

At Home in Circle Valley

While Bob was in prison in Wyoming in 1894, Joseph Rawlins Parker, the thirteenth and last child of the Parker family, was born in Circleville. People might wonder how an outlaw's family members are affected by his reputation. I can remember that even though we lived under a cloud, our lives seemed quite normal.

From time to time, word filtered back by rumor or through the newspapers of the escapades of the Wild Bunch or the Hole-in-the-Wall Gang or the Powder Springs Gang. We never knew for sure whether our brother was deeply involved. Mother and Dad were determined that this blot on our family would not ruin the rest of us. I recall how thoughtful my parents were of each other. For example, if Dad was out in the field, Mother would send one of us with a drink of cool water for him. I can still see that shiny brass bucket we carried it in.

Water was a problem at the ranch. Before we dug our well, we had to use the water from the irrigation ditch. We had hundred-gallon barrels filled with ditch water. We'd cover the barrels with gunnysacks to keep the water cool and let the sediment sink to the bottom. Sometimes the water was so muddy Mother couldn't wash her clothes. Then, instead of using that water, we went up to the Canebrakes, a mile and a half south of the ranch. Mother took her laundry and heated water over an open fire in the boiler and washed up there, with a scrubbing board. We took along a picnic lunch, and most of us played while Mother put out the wash. We never realized how hard it was on her. Then she put the wet clothes in the wagon, drove back to the ranch, and hung them on the line to dry. We always made a day of it.

After our well was dug, what a luxury it was to have cold water pulled by a bucket out of that dark hole. One day the Applegate girls were at the ranch visiting. Mother had a table set outside under the trees just for us.

"Lula, let's get some water for our lunch," Mary Applegate suggested.

I went to the well and found the bucket half full. When I let it down, it pulled me down with it. "Help!" I screamed. Fortunately Mary was close by and caught me by the feet, or I wouldn't be here to tell this story. The well was over eighty feet deep.

We found many ways of enjoying life.

The Sevier River was only a short distance east of the ranch house. Our "vacation resort" was a beautiful shady spot with willows and birches almost meeting over a canal where we went swimming. Sometimes while swimming, if we were in a particularly silly mood, my older sister would baptize us. (Our religion practices baptism by immersion.) But our sacrilegious play would have been frowned on by our elders. If we so much as put up a hand or a toe, down we went again—and again—until we had been completely immersed and came up gasping, screaming and laughing. What fun!

The swimming hole up by the Parker Dam on the Sevier River was also a summer recreation spot. It's no more than a mile south of the ranch. To this day, it's Circleville's swimming "spa" and is called the Parker Hole.

Chokecherrying or gathering serviceberries was another excuse for an outing. Sometimes we wondered what Bob was doing for fun. No doubt his entertainment was more exciting.

During the winter we rode horseback three miles into Circleville to school. When it got too cold, we had to stay in town at Aunt Sarah Morrill's during the week and go home weekends. Invariably my brother Mark (just younger than I) came home weekends with the knees of his trousers worn through, much to Mother's dismay. Mark explained, "It's because we pray so much at Aunt Sarah's; it just wears out my knees." Needless to say, the real reason was playing marbles. That boy played marbles the year 'round.

Mother and her girls sewed carpet rags by the mile, and Aunt Sarah Morrill wove our carpets for us. Over and over Mother washed the wool from our sheep until it was white and soft, then she carded it for bats to put in the quilts. I often helped with this chore. In the evenings while she carded wool, we sang and listened to our parents' stories. Our favorite songs were *Annie Laurie, Way Down in Tennessee, Home, Sweet Home,* and *Hard Times, Come Again No More.* We had an organ which Mother played a little. We all played it a little, but Nina became quite accomplished.

Mother knitted all the stockings for the family and did the sewing for all six of her girls. She knitted wristbands to keep the boys' wrists warm above their gloves in the winter. She worried about Bob. Who was looking after his needs? She mended so skillfully that when the foot of a stocking wore out, she knitted a new bottom and attached it to the upper with a seam on the outside around our feet so it wouldn't irritate.

Of course, we girls also learned to sew. Mother owned the first drop-head Singer sewing machine in town, which I still have. On Sundays we always donned our prettiest dresses and went to church. Mother put our hair up on rags so it would be curled for Sunday. During the week, when we were outside a lot, Mother sewed our bonnets to our hair to keep out the sun. We hated it, but she said, "I can't stand to look at a lot of freckle-faced girls."

One winter Dad took a load of grain to Cedar City to be sold so that he could buy our Christmas gifts there. He got everything he needed for a wonderful Christmas. Situated in Bear Valley was a public camphouse, where people could stop overnight on long journeys from one community to another. It was a small cabin with a door, a window, and a fireplace. I stayed there several times while traveling with Dad.

That particular night he stopped at the camp. There were two other men—strangers—camping there, too. They all cooked their supper on the fireplace and went to bed. Next morning these men got up long before daybreak and left. When Dad went out to put his food in the wagon, he found they had made off with all his Christmas purchases. He was furious, but there was nothing to do but go on home empty-handed. It was too late to try to follow the thieves.

Mother was disappointed, but she always made the best of things. In spite of the pinch, they managed to get something for each of us. She had a lovely tree as always, decorated with a few stars cut out of tin. She made doughnuts; we popped corn and had apples, of course. We had a glorious, happy Christmas. I wonder if those two men did. But how we silently longed to be all together, especially at Christmas. Little did we know how many Christmases Bob brightened by his generosity.

My parents believed Brigham Young when he said it was cheaper to feed the Indians than to fight them. Once when we were at the ranch, a young Indian boy, Jody Crow, came to our place with a bruised leg and ankle. It was probably a bad sprain. Mother took him in and cared for him. She laid on his leg sagebrush packs made by boiling sage; then she used that water to bathe his leg. Afterward she bound the affected part with sage leaves. She continued this for about two weeks before he could walk on it. Goodness knows, there was plenty of sagebrush at our place. It grew at least three or four feet high.

"Why are you so good to a stranger—and even an Indian?" I asked.

Mother replied, "Bread cast upon the waters will return to you. If it was LeRoy who had been hurt, I'd want someone to take care of him the same way." And who knows, perhaps many times it saved us from loss or harm. She never knew how Bob would be the recipient of her "bread cast upon water" at the hands of an Indian woman.

When we lived at the ranch, the Indians often worried us. One day we saw Indians coming toward our place while Mother was in town. They were whooping and yelling. My oldest sister took us over into the brush and said, "You stay down and don't you dare put your heads up!"

She went back to the house, fearing they would burn it down. We were afraid they would get her. But when they reached the house we saw that, instead of being on the warpath, they were drunk on IXL Bitters which they got at the town store. An old red rooster had just died, and lay in the yard. The Indians instantly spotted the rooster and took the feathers from his tail, put them in their hair, and went whooping away.

I've heard it said that tramps used to mark a place where they were given a handout. Our place surely must have been marked, because so many stopped. One day the Applegate girls—Mary and Vinnie—were visiting us. South of the ranch the knoll is high enough to see a long distance down the road. We were playing on the hill when we saw a tramp plodding along. We were scared stiff. Vinnie and Mary were very thin girls; so they slipped into some of our brothers' clothes and hats, stuffing their hair up under the hats. Then they rolled a smoke of bark and sat there against the granary so the tramp would think there were men at the house and wouldn't bother us. Blanche and I gave him a drink of water, and he went on his way. He probably had no intention of harming us, but we felt better with the girls dressed to resemble men.

Our family was great for naming places and animals, and this didn't' stop when our childhood days were over. At one time our team was named Cap and Bill. Another horse was called Sneak, because he could sneak through anything. Old Jack was our mainstay. He pulled the sleigh and the buggy, and we also rode him. At last, at the age of thirty, Old Jack gave up the ghost. Broken-hearted, the kids went up on the hill and worked a couple of days to make a hole big enough and deep enough to bury him so that the coyotes couldn't eat him. Any farm animal deserved a proper burial, we thought.

Uncle Dan and Aunt Sue Gillies lived in Circleville. Occasionally they brought their big family to visit us. What fun we had. At one time there was an epidemic of some kind in Circleville, so Aunt Sue brought her family out to the ranch to avoid the disease. It was such fun that we kids prayed for a long siege. No doubt our parents prayed in reverse. We were disappointed when the plague turned out to be of short duration.

As the family grew, Dad built a large partitioned room for bedrooms on the south and a kitchen on the east so that the kitchen and dining room were together. The original two rooms are still standing. The large room was our living room and the smaller one a bedroom.

Every Christmas Dad and the boys cut down a juniper in the nearby mountains and placed it in the southeast corner of the living room by the fireplace. As I visit there now, I wonder that such a small house contained such a large family. Of course, we were not all there at the same time.

At least once a year part of the family went south to Washington to visit our grandparents and to bring back fruit. We always visited our other relatives in Dixie. My cousin, Camilla Woodbury Judd, told me of her own recollections of our visits to the southern part of the state. She said: "Uncle Max always had such proud, beautiful horses, as they drove up to our place. There were a lot of kids when we all got together and we slept in the yard. When my brothers wore out their pants, Mama cut them off and they became underwear. One time after the Parker family left, my brothers told me the Parker boys didn't wear worn-out pants for underwear. They had white union suits!"

Never once that I know of did our relatives bring up Butch's name. But I'm sure they shared our heartache in silence.

On one of these trips to Dixie, when I was about thirteen, I stayed with Grandpa and Grandma Parker for the better part of the year. At first, I was terribly homesick. Often we walked up through the lot to Aunt Ellen's to keep me from crying in the evening. Playing with her children, and especially Theresa, soon drove away the homesickness.

There was no bank in town, so Grandfather brought home a little sack which contained the store's earnings for the day. I snickered as I watched him hide it in a sack of carpet rags by Grandma's sewing machine. "No one would ever think of looking for money in a bag of rags," he winked.

I think every writer who has written about Butch Cassidy has had Grandfather Robert Parker die crossing the plains in the bitter cold of winter and the poor Widow Parker being left to raise her children in American Fork; some say Spanish Fork. Nothing could be further from the truth. As I explained in chapter two, they walked across the plains and mountains in the summer heat, moved to American Fork, then to Beaver, then to Washington, Utah. Grandfather died in 1901 at the age of eighty-one, and Grandmother Parker died earlier—in 1899. They are buried side by side in the cemetery at Washington, Utah.

At home again after our trips to Washington to visit our grandparents, we relished the fruits we brought back, especially the raisins dried in bunches on the stems that we picked for Mother to use in her cooking. We counted each raisin, and the tenth we called a tithing raisin, which we mischievously popped into our mouths. Tithing is a part of our religion, and a tenth of our income is supposed to go to the bishop. Tithing used to be paid in kind: the tenth egg, or sheep, or bale of hay, but it is now paid in cash. Of course, there were those who complained at the supposed burden of tithing, claiming it was not always properly administered by the bishop. My brothers kidded Dad about paying his tithing so faithfully. Dad said, "By gum, the only ones I ever heard kick about it are those who never paid a dime."

But my parents' charity didn't stop at tithing; and their help was always given quietly. One day Annie Wixom stopped me on the street. She was a widow, having a very hard time getting along. "Who do you think left a ham on my doorstep this morning?" she asked.

"The bishop, I guess," I replied.

"Don't you believe it. It was your father."

"How do you know?"

She winked, "I saw him hurrying out the gate— thought I wouldn't see him."

Another neighbor, Mrs. Mansor, told me that my father and brothers kept her in meat. Her daughter, Arilla, who used to clean the house for Dad, told me one day at the cemetery: "Lula, your father was the only one who ever paid me more for working than I asked."

Bob inherited their generosity.

Mother never turned anyone away hungry. Some of the men who came to our door were good and some were bad. One evening Mother was home alone with just the smaller children when a tramp knocked on the door. He was wearing a wide-brimmed hat, laced with tiny strips of leather. Mother was uneasy and wouldn't let him stay. She watched him trudge down the road southward. Her conscience got the best of her. "Eb, you go bring that poor fellow back here," she said. "He must be starved. He's some mother's son." When he returned, she fed him and let him sleep in the granary.

When the granary finally did burn down, it wasn't the fault of a tramp sleeping there. It was my fault.

We stored books in the granary, and one night Blanche and I lighted a candle and went out to find a book to read. I was about ten at the time. I put the candle on a high shelf so that its rays would give a wide light. We were examining the books intently and failed to notice that the candle flame had ignited the leaves poking through the top of the shed. The wood, very dry, quickly burst into flames. Mother and Dad rushed from the house and couldn't even get the harnesses out in time. They drenched Mother's quilts and threw them over the haystack to keep it from catching fire. Unfortunately, a cat with her kittens had made her home in the granary. The cat escaped, but the little kittens were burned, and we were heartbroken.

Also stored in the granary was a barrel of meat and a barrel of molasses. We later joked about having a good supply of molasses candy without having to cook it. The grain smoldered for days, and so did my conscience. The morning after the fire Mrs. Fox, a dear friend, brought a roll of butter that looked so good because we had little food left, most of our supplies having been burned.

Dad remarked that in times past he had worried about Bob burning down the granary with his secret smokes, but he had never dreamed one of his girls would do it.

Eb was in Beaver at school, but he became so homesick he headed for home on horseback in the winter. Although he should never have started out like that, he couldn't stay away any longer. The snow was deep, and darkness closed in on him. He stopped and made a fire from the little wood he could find. In the freezing cold, he dozed frequently and would have been content to slip away. But a voice which sounded strangely like Mother's kept rousing him until at daybreak he could continue on his way home. Even thought it hurt him terribly to "thaw out," he was grateful to be home. No matter how young or old, we've all been homebodies. Mother often wondered why Bob's great love for her didn't carry her anxious voice to him at critical times to keep him from going the wrong way.

Our place became a stop-off for travelers. Our house was on the east of the property. Mother's vegetable and flower garden was west of the house, with a few fruit trees—pears and apples. It was a beautiful oasis. There were the cottonwoods and the stately poplars which Bob had helped to plant. The ditch ran to the west. Between the ditch and the road, Dad kept a campground where people could stop for the night as they were passing through. Dad was paid 25¢ a night for feeding a team for the campers. Mother sold them bread and vegetables, milk and butter as they needed them. This brought in a little extra cash.

In those days the old road was west of our house and yard instead of to the east as it is today. The hills sloped upward in the west, dotted with bluebells. In those hills Dad and the boys pastured their stock.

Mother was very wise. Her girls were never taught to milk cows. If we didn't know how to milk, she maintained, the boys knew they had to be home to take care of that chore. That was one thing which built dependability and kept them at our fireside.

We had fun around the table in the evenings— working, joking, laughing, and singing. But Mother wouldn't tolerate profanity. One evening Dan ripped out an oath. Quick as your next breath, Mother clapped her hand over his mouth. He apologized to her. But that didn't keep the boys from cussing when she wasn't around.

How we adored little Joseph Rawlins, the last of our brood. When he was a little tyke, my sister Nina had typhoid fever. At that time typhoid was truly a dread disease. She was over the worst of it when a woman from southern Utah came by, bringing a gift from one of Mother's friends—a little Dixie wine for medicinal purposes. The traveling woman was selling peach preserves made with molasses. Of course, Mother courteously bought a jar of the preserves. The woman told Mother her sick daughter would recover faster if she would give her a little wine.

Suddenly Mother interrupted their conversation, realizing that little Joseph Rawlins had disappeared. She was frantic. She rushed across the field to the irrigation canal, and sure enough, the stick horse which Rawlins always rode was lying by the narrow foot bridge. Mother screamed for Dad. He waded into the canal and on downstream, running his arms through the muddy water in search of the little boy. In a short time the neighbors were there to help. Jess Applegate walked up between the canal and the dam. In that narrowing slice of land, little Rawlins squatted on his heels, intent on a cornered bobcat. Rawlins was creeping closer and closer, as he coaxed, "Here, kitty-kitty-kitty."

During all this excitement, my sister took a big drink of the Dixie wine. Sure enough, it did help, and she recovered rapidly.

We nicknamed Joseph Rawlins "Cub." As a child, he was quite an artist. One day at school the teacher asked the students to write a composition or a story. After allowing sufficient time for the writing, he scanned the class to see who should read his story first. Rawlins's head was bent over his paper in concentration. The teacher said, "Rawlins, you've been so busy, I'd wager you have a good story. Let's hear it."

Rawlins stood up. With eyes glued to his paper, Rawlins read a very exciting story. The teacher remarked enthusiastically, "That's an excellent story, Rawlins. I'd like to keep it." He walked down the aisle to Rawlins's desk and picked up his paper. But all he could see was a very good sketch of a beautiful horse. Rawlins had told his exciting story from that picture—a real picture story.

As Rawlins grew up, he sometimes drank "with the boys." Our sheriff kept such a close check on the boys in town, that he would actually come up close to them and sniff their breath. One day Rawlins cleaned up to go downtown. He knew he would meet the sheriff; so he filled his mouth with garlic and made it a point to wobble suspiciously. When the sheriff came close to smell, Rawlins opened his mouth wide and gave him a good whiff! Then it was the sheriff's turn to wobble.

When I was in my teens, we moved into Circleville into a lovely brick house with two stories. On the main floor was a living room, a bedroom, and a kitchen. Mother was the proud possessor of a beautiful Home Comfort stove. Upstairs were three large bedrooms. The stairs were extremely steep, and we always climbed up and down

My youngest brother, Joseph Rawlins Parker, nicknamed Cub, who looked like our brother, Robert LeRoy. They both resembled Mother.

236

with great caution. In our town there was no more than one house on each corner of the block, which gave us lots of breathing room. Dad and the boys continued to farm the ranch property and maintained the stock out there.

In those days, our newspaper came out twice a week. Occasionally there would be a note about some escapade of the Wild Bunch or the Hole-in-the-Wall Gang, or sometimes they were called Butch Cassidy's gang; at least Butch was usually given credit for it, no matter who did it. We were humiliated and embarrassed and wished we didn't have to face the townspeople. Mother would rather have stayed home, but for the sake of her children, she forced herself to continue teaching in the church. She always wore a pleasant expression, and no one dreamed the weight she carried inside.

We had family prayers together, kneeling at our chairs around the table. If I live to be two hundred, I will always remember Mother's fervent prayers, pleading with God to turn her boy around and bring him home safely, that he might go straight.

The following two appendices are included here, not because they are full of incidents involving my brother, Butch Cassidy (they are not), but because they reveal something about the people who were Butch's closest friends while he was an outlaw.

If the overworked axiom, "Water seeks its own level," can be applied here, we can gain a little better insight into Butch's character by becoming more familiar with the lives of some of the people he chose to associate with—the Bassett family and Elzy Lay.

The Bassetts
Appendix A

Josephine (Josie) and Ann Bassett were daughters of Herbert and Mary Eliza Chamberlain Bassett, early Brown's Park settlers.

Josie was the elder Bassett girl and was a lifetime friend of Butch Cassidy and Elzy Lay. Ann, a would-be cowgirl, dogged their footsteps, trying to learn every possible cowboy trick from them. Extremely imaginative, she often found difficulty separating fact from her own dream world. Her eager listeners never went away without a good story, which they assumed to be first-person fact.

On occasion, when a particularly lurid article appeared in print about the Bassetts—and many did—Josie fumed, "Ann, why do you tell such lies?"

Invariably Ann replied, "They don't want the truth—they want a good story. So I gave it to them."

"But don't you realize? The things you say are recorded and become history. Then no one will ever believe the truth as it really is!" How right she was. Charles Kelly made the most of her vivid imagination, and other writers have added to it.

The statistical information herein is from Herbert Bassett's personally kept red record book and is substantiated by entries in the 1892 census of Hot Springs County, Arkansas.

Herbert Bassett was born July 31, 1834, at Brownsville, Jefferson County, New York. After college, he taught school in Illinois until Abraham Lincoln called for his 300,000 soldiers, and Herbert enlisted in the Union Army in 1861 in Company "K" of the Ohio Volunteers. Following his mustering out, he became Collector of Revenue in Norfolk, Virginia, where he met and married Mary Eliza Chamberlain on September 21, 1871. Eliza was born on August 28, 1857. At the death of her parents, when she was very young, Eliza and her sister Hannah went to live with their maternal grandparents whose name was Crawford. Eliza was only fourteen when she married Herbert, who was thirty-seven. Contrary to the usual printed report, Herbert Bassett was a most engaging, dynamic man. He had to have been to claim the heart of Mary Eliza Chamberlain, for she had a captivating personality with understanding and acumen far beyond her years.

The couple moved to Rockport, Hot Springs County, Arkansas. Because Herbert was well educated, he always had lucrative employment. Josie was born on January 17, 1874, in Rockport, and Sam was born there on October 30, 1876.

But Herbert Bassett suffered from asthma. At the suggestion of his brother Sam, who had already gone West, he decided to move to the western mountain country. With the two children, Herbert and Mary Eliza headed for Wyoming, where Herbert worked for a short while as a bookkeeper for a mercantile firm, A. C. Beckwith & Company, in Evanston. Later, by way of Rock Springs, they arrived with their loaded wagons in Brown's Hole. They also brought a negro "mammy" with them for Sam, who had been an incubator baby. Mary Eliza was so impressed with the beauty of Brown's Hole that she insisted it be called Brown's Park.

Other children were born after the Bassetts arrived in Brown's Park: Ann—May 12, 1878; Elbert (Eb)—June 21, 1880, born at Green River City, Wyoming; George—March 29, 1884, in Brown's Park.

Ann, the first baby born in Brown's Park, thrived on the early attention, and all her life she demanded, and received, center stage. Perhaps it was this desire for attention that made it easy for her to tell a good "story."

The Bassett home was the chief meeting place for the Park, and Herbert Bassett was the preacher-of-sorts in the area. Although he had never been trained for the clergy, he conducted informal nondenominational services on Sundays. Herbert had a fine library. He was a congenial, sociable man, and an excellent conversationalist with eyes that looked through the sham of a man. Of Elzy Lay he said, "There is a boy who missed his calling. He's got no business robbing trains and stealing horses. He should be in some honorable profession."

Herbert was also the postmaster; the small post office was adjacent to the Bassett house.

Herbert's health was not good, but his wife was an energetic, intelligent young woman, capable of strenuous physical labor, who knew how to get things done. So it was quite natural that she was the boss of the ranch.

At first the Bassett girls didn't realize that many of the cowboys who came and went were hunted criminals evading the law. They seemed to be like anyone else and were treated in the same way.

Herbert Bassett insisted that his daughters have the meager education afforded by the local school that held classes for all of three months. Later, Josie went to school in Craig, Colorado, then spent 2½ years at the St. Mary's-of-the-Wasatch in Salt Lake City, Utah, a Catholic girls' school. While she was attending St. Mary's, her mother died of appendicitis on December 11, 1892, at the early age of thirty-five, and Josie stayed home with her father after that. He was lost without his wife.

Ann went to Rock Springs to school, then spent a year at St. Mary's, but she refused to go back. She did not go to the finishing school in Boston, as has been published. She traveled a good bit, but her polish came simply from using to advantage the training of a good home.

Ann first married Hi Bernard, foreman of the Haley 2-Bar outfit. They were divorced. Later she married Frank Willis, who survived her by many years. While living in Leeds, Utah, she frequently visited with her close friend, who was our Aunt Ada Parker McMullen. Ann had much to tell about Butch Cassidy, whom she always classed as one of her best friends. Ann died in Leeds on May 10, 1956, at the age of seventy-eight.

Ann's first love had been Matt Rash, who was murdered by Tom Horn, a hired killer of the big cattlemen, including Ora Haley. She was later arrested, tried, and acquitted for killing a cow that was supposed to have belonged to Ora Haley. This sensational trial continued for years and cost Haley many, many thousands of dollars and the taxpayers a lot more.

Ann got the title of Queen Ann one day when a newsman got the best of her quick temper. She flew into a rage and refused to give him any information. He dubbed her Queen Ann because she was so high and mighty. The name stuck—Queen Ann, Queen of the Cattle Rustlers.

It has been said that Butch Cassidy courted Josie. When her son Crawford asked her if she ever went out with Butch, she just looked wise and smiled. The Bassetts found it hard to believe that Butch was an outlaw.

Josie was unfortunate at marriage. She married Jim MacKnight first. On page 81 of his book, *The Outlaw Trail*, Charles Kelly says that Josie married Jim MacKnight, "but later kicked him out and emphasized her remarks by shooting MacKnight, who departed suddenly with a leaden souvenir." She was also given the dubious credit of poisoning another husband. This illustrates very clearly how writers have twisted so-called facts. On file in the Dinosaur National Monument at Jensen, Utah, is a tape of an interview Murl Messersmith had with Josie. The following dialogue is a part of that tape:

JOSIE: I disagreed with him [Jim MacKnight] because he was on the wrong track, I thought. I didn't like that whiskey business. . . . I said we live in two different worlds; you go your way and I'll stay at home, and I did. . . . We never had any more fuss.

MESSERSMITH: *That discredits the stories, then, that I've heard.*

JOSIE: *The stories I've read, why, the most ridiculous fool things I ever read anyway. Who do you suppose it finally came from? That Charles Kelly said that I shot him. Well, he [Jim] was quite an active man for a dead man. He got married and had five children. And someone else, some other paper, said I hired a young man twenty-two years old to shoot.*

Of the shooting of Jim MacKnight, Crawford MacKnight had this to say:

Dad kinda kidnapped me and my brother, took us to Salt Lake and then up to Smithfield and turned us over to old Aunt Jodie Heath. Well, Mother wanted us kids brought home, naturally, and she had papers made out, and they deputized a little guy in Rock Springs to come out to serve papers and a warrant for his arrest and a subpoena to appear in court. My Dad wouldn't accept service.

He said, "To hell with it." He tore the papers up and handed them back to Bill Harris and said, "Bill, you know what you can do with these papers." And he told him what it was possible to do with them. He agreed right there to go to court. Well, that was about all there was to it. But he turned and walked off, and Bill Harris shot him right between the shoulders with a .38 pistol, a little old bulldog. Of course, Dad had to go to Salt Lake to a hospital by team and buggy. They couldn't remove the bullet. Dad packed that old .38 slug in his back, buried in him. Old Aunt Jodie got us kids back down to Salt Lake. Grandfather Bassett and Mother appeared, and the kids were in evidence, and Dad surrendered us kids.

Mother didn't like Dad. He didn't like her, but there was never any real bad blood between them.

Josie was married three more times: to Charlie Cranney, who died of a heart condition, to Emerson Wells, who also died, and to Ben Morris, whom she divorced.

When Crawford questioned his mother about her poisoning one of her husbands, she simply exploded, "Why do people tell such lies!" And he knew better than to press the questioning.

Josie had only two sons, Crawford and Herbert "Chick" MacKnight. She took care of her father until he decided he wanted to see the country. He spent his last years traveling around, visiting the Old Soldier Homes, and reminiscing. He died on July 30, 1918, in the National Soldiers Home in Quincy, Illinois, and is buried there.

At about sixty-one, Josie was arrested by two local cattlemen for cattle rustling. In reality, the cattlemen wanted her removed from the premises for the purpose of jumping her homestead, a choice piece of property with good water rights.

They planned their case against her carefully, concealing hides they had pieced together so that the brands would match. At the end of the long trial, the jury refuted the evidence, and the case was thrown out of court. Attorney's fees were high. Crawford and Flossie, his wife, had to sell Flossie's inherited land to pay those costs. But Josie meant so much to Flossie that she was willing to do this to save the property and reputation of her mother-in-law.

In 1973, with one of Josie's granddaughters, a daughter of Crawford and Flossie MacKnight, we visited Josie's cabin at Cub Creek. With the shadows of the towering cliffs as her backdrop, across the swift Green River and about fourteen miles from Jensen, Josie built her sturdy cabin. The property is now owned and neglected by the Parks Department. As we walked approximately a mile from the road to the tumble-down house, Dottie Mac-Knight Burnham pointed out the lay of the land as it was when she spent considerable time with "Granny Josie." With a wave of her hand she indicated where the garden had flourished, the flowers and fruits, her ingenious irrigation system. Dottie pulled watercress from the creek for us. She talked with nostalgic animation to cover the persistent catch in her voice.

Josie Bassett Morris in front of her cabin at Cub Creek. *Courtesy of the* Vernal Express.

The hewn-log walls of the house still stand. The house is a shambles, wrecked by vandals, but Dottie lovingly explained where each piece of furniture had once stood. The house had been clean and cozy. Josie slept, summer and bitter winter, on the enclosed screened and vine-covered porch. Scarlet poppies had bloomed in the yard.

Leaving the house, we wandered out the back way and found Josie's fitted-stone storage cellar in excellent condition. A few dusty bottles remained on the shelves.

In that isolated spot Josie lived almost until her death.

At the age of seventy-nine Josie was the queen of the rodeo in the Vernal July 24 celebration. She rode the parade route in an old-time buggy with Averill Harriman, who was campaigning for the presidency of the United States that year. At the rodeo, she made the grand entry astride a pinto pony just behind the American flag. As she stood proudly in the stirrups, waving her Stetson, the cheering crowd rose in a body to honor a grand old lady.

Two days before Christmas, it was cold, slick, and wet, and Josie walked out to the spring, carrying her water bucket. Old Helen, her devoted horse of twenty years, thought she was bringing a bucket of oats. In her eagerness, she knocked Josie over, breaking her leg. Josie dragged herself back into the house, although it was quite a distance. She had only two chunks of coal by the fireplace. She threw one on the fire and the other a little later, realizing it was her last source of warmth in the house. Aware that she had no water, she crawled back outside and scooped up a pan full of snow. Inside again, she pulled a blanket off the couch and bundled up close to the fireplace, prone on the floor. There she stayed all day and night.

The next day Crawford and his daughter Willda drove over in the old car to get Josie to spend Christmas with them, as usual. They stopped along the way to pick up firewood, in no hurry. Suddenly Crawford said, "Willda, I've got a funny feeling."

246

"Me too. Something's wrong at Granny's," Willda agreed.

They drove closer where they could see the house in the distance. No smoke curled from the chimney. Crawford knew something was wrong, and they hurried as fast as the ice and snow would permit.

Crawford opened the door and peered inside, to see a lumpy blanket in front of the fireplace and a shock of white hair emerging from one end. His heart sank. The sound of the squeaky hinge roused Josie, and she raised herself slightly, quavering, "That you, Crawford?"

After they had built a good fire and warmed some soup, Willda stayed with Josie while Crawford went back to town to get a station wagon to move her to the hospital in Salt Lake City. She was transferred to St. Mark's Hospital there. What a Christmas!

Dr. Lamb performed surgery on her hip and pinned it but warned her family she would probably never walk again. Incredibly, on the thirteenth day Josie walked out of the hospital with the aid of a walker and went to Crawford's house to receive Flossie's care all winter and into the spring.

Josie was eager to return to her own rustic home and assured them she was fine and could take care of herself. But soon Crawford and Flossie noticed she seemed to be swelling with fluid. So they took her back to Salt Lake City to the doctor. She stayed at her granddaughter's house for three weeks in order to be under the doctor's surveillance. She was alone there when she died on May 1, 1964, of heart failure.

Most of her life she had either lived alone or some of her grandchildren willingly stayed with her. They all adored her. Crawford's wife Flossie always called her "Mother," and she loved her as a mother. Theirs was a close relationship through the years.

Crawford thought perhaps they shouldn't have a funeral. After all, even though Josie had been brought up by devout Christian parents, she wasn't baptized "anything." The Mormon bishop offered the Jensen Ward House for the services, and he conducted the service. One granddaughter played the organ for the services, and Dottie and her husband sang. Josie would have liked that. No one was more surprised than Crawford to see the chapel bursting and overflowing, with many unable to get inside. Following the service, the funeral cortege drove the one hundred miles to the original Bassett ranch in Brown's Park for burial. The family was shocked but pleased to see a large group waiting at the graveside to pay their last respects to a great lady. They had traveled from Craig, Colorado, and Rock Springs, Wyoming, from Washington State, Virginia, Texas, from Boston, and from sections of Utah. Her body was laid to rest, but the printed lies continue.

If much of this information seems biased, remember that my source is Josie herself and members of her family who knew her best.

Elzy Lay
Appendix B

The following is an interview given to Dora Flack by Harvey Lay Murdock, son of Marvel Lay Murdock and grandson of Elzy Lay, on April 11, 1972, in his office in Salt Lake City, Utah. In a separate interview on June 6, 1972, at her home in Heber City, Utah, Marvel Lay Murdock added some details.

Harvey refers to his grandparents as Elzy and Maude for clarity. He never knew his grandfather well enough to use the familiar term Grandpa.

"When I first met Josie Bassett Morris, it was one of those cases that you procrastinate for years. One day I was in Vernal, and I thought I'd better go see her.

"I went to the Park Ranger and he directed me on a map. I followed this and got up to her place. I knew I must be lost. There was no sign of life. I was turning my car around in the yard when I saw Josie walking toward the house with a bucket of water. She was dressed in a pair of old bib overalls and had a man's hat on. She was eighty-six years old then.

"I asked, 'Did you ever know Elzy Lay?' She looked at me several seconds. I was extremely conscious of her searching look as she studied me. That name brought back many memories to her.

"She said, 'You must be Marvel's boy.' I told her I was.

" 'Come in and talk to me. Elzy Lay was the finest gentleman I have ever had the pleasure of knowing.'

Elzy Lay, taken about the time he was married to Maude Davis in 1896. *Courtesy of Mrs. J. T. (Marvel) Murdock, Heber, Utah.*

"We went in, and she had a guest book there which I signed immediately, and then she told me many things that went on. It was amazing to me that this woman was such a soft, pleasant person. She was like a grandmother, so warm. I had gone up with misgivings. I had heard stories of her running a husband off with a gun, trying to poison another, and being arrested for borrowing cattle from somebody else. I didn't know but what she would run me off. So I was indeed surprised when I found her so pleasant.

"Some of the things she told me led me to believe that she was in love with Elzy Lay. She talked about him constantly—what a fine man he was. She told me of going to dances with him down in Brown's Park. She would continually mention the temperance of both him and Butch. She said they were a little too wise to get liquored up too much and get mouthy. They needed to keep their identity as closely covered as possible and yet still live, and hide their whereabouts. . . .

"When Elzy Lay was just a youngster in Ohio, he ran around with a boy named William McGinnis. He and young Bill McGinnis left home because it seemed Lay was in love with a local girl, and both parents felt they were too young. William McGinnis returned home after a while, but Lay stayed in the west.

"As he was going through this part of the country [Wyoming, Colorado, and eastern Utah] he did ranch work around Brown's Park and then ran into Matt Warner. He worked for Matt mavericking cattle and breaking horses, and so forth. For quite a few summers, Lay put up hay and did general farm and range work around Brown's Park. He worked for the Bassetts and also for Charlie Crouse two summers. It was from Charlie Crouse he learned his skill as a horseman.

"I don't know just how Butch and Lay got acquainted. They didn't know each other before Butch had been in prison. They complemented one another. . . .

"One of the first jobs was the Montpelier Bank robbery to raise money to get Matt Warner off. . . .

"The winter of 1896-97, they planned and trained to take the Castle Gate Coal payroll. Elzy's wife Maude spent that winter at Robbers' Roost. . . . He was deeply in love with Maude, and she objected strenuously to his way of life.

"Before the Folsom train robbery, Lay worked on the WS Ranch near Alma, New Mexico, with Mr. French. In the gun battle following the train robbery between the outlaws and the posse, Sheriff Farr and one or two others of the posse were killed. Subsequently, Lay was captured and sentenced to the New Mexico State Penitentiary for murder and armed robbery. He was sentenced under the name of William McGinnis # PNM 1348 on October 10, 1899, for a life term, Colfax County, Raton, New Mexico.

"While Lay was in prison, he definitely decided to give up his outlawry, and he decided he was going to make the best of his imprisonment. He became the model prisoner. Lay was pardoned January 10, 1906, by Governor Otero. I wrote to the prison to get details, but they said they didn't have any, just the date of his release.

"Lay returned to Vernal, hoping to be reunited with Maude. However, before finding her, he learned from Cora McCandrus that she had divorced him for desertion. Their daughter Marvel, my mother, was born August 6, 1897, just a few months after the Castle Gate robbery. Maude obtained work with the first newspaper in Vernal, *The Uintah Papoose*. By the time Elzy returned, she had remarried. Broken-hearted, Lay left without seeing the girl he had never quit loving.

"Using the alias of William McGinnis, Lay drifted into Wyoming and obtained work on the Calvert Ranch near Baggs, Wyoming, where he married the boss's daughter, Mary Calvert. Lay was a good deal older than Mary. They had a son and a daughter. He managed the Calvert Ranch but became very discouraged with it. Perhaps it wasn't exciting enough.

"Then he got interested in oil geology through Louie Maupin, a Baggs banker, who had entered an oil prospecting venture with Wiff Wilson and John Crappo, a geologist in the Baggs area. Lay was a good cook and out-doorsman and was hired to join them. He and the geologist headed for the vast desolate rock areas. At the geologist's request, Mr. Maupin ordered several books on oil geology and they were delivered to Lay. The venture was given up because of high expense. Lay went into northern Colorado and eastern Utah, and he discovered what he knew was a large oil find.

"He pulled out, went back to tell Maupin about it, and they went down and staked it out. They proved up on it for two or three years, but Maupin lost interest. Lay was the first to stake out the site of the Hiawatha Oil. Their equipment wouldn't let them go deep enough and they stopped, not knowing that two hundred feet deeper was their desired goal. They had run out of money and the laws had changed. This was done under the Placer Mining Act to begin with. They lost their holdings. It is now leased by Mountain Fuel Supply Company and is owned by Standard Oil Company of California. The records show William McGinnis (Elzy Lay) to be the original oil claimer.

"Lay had sunk everything he owned into the venture, along with money of some of his friends. He felt he had really botched up his life for the second time: first, with Maude and his outlaw career which had brought him nothing but trouble, and now he had failed to make good in oil. He couldn't face Mary. In desperation he tried to run away from it all and went to California. A couple or three years later some people from Wyoming spotted him there. His health was failing.

"These Wyomingites went back home and got in touch with Mary. She picked up her son and daughter and went to California and found him. She was completely devoted to him and nursed him back to health, and he lived a full life after that. He was head of the irrigation system for the Imperial Valley Canal Company.

"While Governor Otero was still serving in New Mexico, he had written to Lay asking him to be the U.S. Marshall, but he declined. Lay didn't think that would be right after his outlaw life."

Elzy Lay and his family in Kansas, August, 1921. Elzy is the man in the white shirt. His daughter Marvel is holding her daughter, Audrey. *Courtesy of Mrs. H. T. (Marvel) Murdock, Heber, Utah.*

When Marvel Lay was fourteen, Elzy came to Vernal to see her at the time of her graduation from Wilcox Academy. She relates her feelings about that meeting:

If I had met him on the street, I would have known him because of the feeling of love that overwhelmed me. He was my father, and I loved him, even if I didn't know him. I didn't know until years later that my father was an outlaw. No one, not Mother or Grandma, had ever told me a thing about it, not at school, nor anywhere. Mother had never said anything except what a fine man he was. He stayed a couple of weeks at that time in Vernal visiting with me.

After he had been there the first time, he thought the hills around Vernal and the rock formations there possibly had oil deposits. But I never saw him again until he came to the ranch out on the Upper Duchesne and my first girl was 2½ years old. This was in 1921. In August of that year, my father came with Mary and their son and daughter. He took me and my little girl, Audrey, and we went back to Woodruff, Kansas, to see his parents. They were the salt of the earth and were respected and loved. They had been a deeply religious family.

Harvey reveals here a little more about his grandfather's relationship with Butch Cassidy:

"It was probably in the summer of 1929 that Lay arrived at the Murdock Ranch in Wolf Creek, Utah, to visit Mother again. He was still interested in geology. Two men came to the ranch in a car. This was Elzy Lay and an oil man on their way to Baggs, Wyoming.

"The day I visited Josie in her log house near the Green River, I challenged her and said, 'You know very well Butch was killed in South America.'

"She replied, 'I know Butch Cassidy a hell of a

lot better than I know you. He was here in Baggs in about 1930.'

"Four different times I challenged her, and she repeated the story in almost the same words every time.

"I talked to Minnie Crouse Rasmussen a year ago. While Butch and Lay were working for her dad in Brown's Park, she was away at school. She knew them when she was about ten years old. After she came back, she saw Lay several times and Butch once after he returned. But she was in Iowa much of the time with her uncle.

"Lay apparently didn't tell Mary much about his life. Zane Grey had approached him about doing a book. He said, 'I don't want to give it to you because I would have to tell the truth and it would hurt innocent people.' But at the last he said, 'Mary, get hold of Zane because I'm not going to live much longer.' Zane Grey lived on Catalina Island. Lay had retired to Los Angeles. He was sick off and on for three years before he died on November 10, 1934, and was buried in Forest Lawn Cemetery in Glendale, California. He died before the writer could get the facts.

"Mother remembers her father as a crack shot. She claims she saw him throw a can in the air and keep it there with his six-shooter."

To the foregoing Marvel Lay Murdock adds a touching bit about the unusual relationship which existed between Elzy Lay, Maude Davis, and Mary Calvert. Maude lived with her daughter, Marvel, the last four years of her life. Marvel relates the details of her mother's death:

My mother loved my father till the day she died. I adored Mary. She was the most loyal person I have ever known. We used to visit with them when I would go to California. They came here to visit before and after my father's death. Several years after my father passed away, Mary was here visiting. Mama got up and ate her breakfast. She seemed fine. I was outside hanging clothes. I remember that I had a bed of pansies right under her bedroom window. When I went outside, she was laughing and joking with Mary. She was so little and thin and wrinkled. She said, "It don't matter to get thin when you're so old and don't care."

As I was hanging the clothes, I heard her call, "Marvel!" I sensed an urgency in her voice. Her heart was bad. I rushed in and made her comfortable.

Mama said, "Mary, I've always loved you for how good you've been to my daughter."

Mary replied, "I've always loved you too, Maude."

"And we loved the same man," Mama smiled. She died a few minutes later. That was July 22, 1958.

As has been indicated by Marvel Murdock, her father's outlaw experiences were kept very quiet, nor did they talk about Butch Cassidy very much. This was the past they all wanted to forget.

However, Butch and Elzy were well known in Vernal by many people. Mrs. Cora McAndrus told Marvel that everybody out there was "stuck on Butch Cassidy."

Marvel said, "My father said Butch wasn't a woman chaser and a drunkard like he was pictured."

When my brother came home, he told us that he considered Elzy Lay to be the best friend he had, that he was a man of his word and was always dependable. Their friendship continued after both of them forsook the outlaw life.

Bibliography

Burroughs, John Rolfe. *Where the Old West Stayed Young.* New York: Bonanza Books.

1880 Census of the State of Utah. Microfilm. Utah Historical Society, Salt Lake City, Utah.

"Bold Outlaws Get $7,000 in Gold." *Eastern Utah Advocate,* 22 April 1897.

Deseret News. Salt Lake City, 25 July 1970.

Family records kept by Maximillian Parker.

Fremont County Court Records, Lander, Wyoming.

Hafen, LeRoy R. and Ann W. *Handcarts to Zion.* Glendale, California: The Arthur H. Clark Co., 1960.

Hayden, Willard C. "Butch Cassidy and the Great Montpelier Bank Robbery." *Idaho Yesterdays* 15 (Spring 1971): 1.

Horan, James D. *Desperate Men.* New York: Doubleday & Co.

Horan, James D., and Sann, Paul. *Pictorial History of the Wild West.* New York: Crown Publishers.

Journal History. Emigration Records. Salt Lake City: LDS Church Historical Department.

Kelly, Charles. *The Outlaw Trail.* Salt Lake City: Charles Kelly, 1938.

Records of the Genealogical Society. The Church of Jesus Christ of Latter-day Saints. Salt Lake City, Utah.

Warner, Matt, and King, Murray E. *The Last of the Bandit Riders.* Caldwell, Idaho: The Caxton Printers, Ltd., 1940.

Wells, Governor Heber M. Correspondence files. Utah State Archives. Salt Lake City.

Index

*Relationship to Robert LeRoy Parker (alias Butch Cassidy).

*Relationship to Robert LeRoy Parker (alias Butch Cassidy).

M

N

O

P

*Relationship to Robert LeRoy Parker (alias Butch Cassidy).

June 24th 1893 at 10 oclock A.M. this cause coming on for hearing the Defendants each appear in person and by their said attorney C. J. Rathbone. M. C Brown appears as [illegible] Defendants now each in person and for himself states to the court that they now waive all further examination respecting said charge and submit the matter to the court for its further orders in the premises and the court now being fully advised, thereupon. it is ordered that the defendants each be held to answer to said charge at the next term of the District Court to be held in said County, that they each are required to give bail in the sum of four hundred dollars for their appearance and to so answer at said term of said District Court as required by law, and in default of said bail they be and stand committed to the jail of said County until discharged therefrom by due course of law, and it is further ordered that the witnesses present on the part of the state do each give their own recognizance for their appearance at said term as required by law and in default thereof to be and stand committed. Defendants now each give recognizance as required by said order with Leonard Short and Eli A. Signor as their sureties thereon and the same being filed and approved by me they are released from custody and the witnesses present James Thomas, David Stewart, Otto France, John W. Chapman and David Blanchard give their recognizances as required by said order and the same is filed and approved by me

Charly Allen
Justice of the Peace